This book is a modern adaptation for children of William Shakespeare's "The Merry Wives of Windsor," which is a work in the public domain. While the original story and characters are based on Shakespeare's play, this adaptation includes significant original content tailored for a young audience. These additions include simplified language and reimagined scenes, specifically created to make this timeless tale accessible and engaging for young readers. The intention of this adaptation is to introduce children to the classic story in a manner that respects the essence of Shakespeare's original work, while presenting it in a way that is relatable and understandable for a younger audience.

THE MERRY WIVES OF WINDSOR

SHAKESPEARE FOR KIDS

JEANETTE VIGON

"We can say of Shakespeare, that never has a man turned so little knowledge to such great account."

— T. S. ELIOT

WHY I WROTE THIS BOOK THE WAY I DID

When I embarked on the journey of adapting Shakespeare's plays for children, my primary goal was to bridge the gap between the timeless allure of Shakespeare's narratives and the imaginative worlds of young readers. The decision to adapt these plays for children was driven by a desire to introduce them to the richness of literary classics at an early age, fostering a love for literature that could grow with them.

Choosing to maintain the original structure of acts and scenes was a deliberate effort to preserve the integrity and rhythm of Shakespeare's works. This approach not only honors the original compositions but also introduces young readers to the conventions of drama and the beauty of structured story-telling. It was important to me that children experience the plays as they were intended, albeit in a more accessible form.

Incorporating literary language while ensuring it remains engaging and understandable for children was a balancing act. I aimed to simplify the complexity of Shakespeare's language without diluting its power and beauty. By carefully selecting vocabulary and crafting sentences that convey the essence of the original plays, I aspired to captivate young minds and stimulate their intellectual curiosity.

Adapting these plays also involved making thoughtful choices about content, ensuring that themes and scenes were appropriate for a young audience. This required a sensitive approach to storytelling, where the lessons of love, loyalty, betrayal, and justice are presented in a manner that is both educational and entertaining.

In summary, the creation of this book was a labor of love, guided by the belief that Shakespeare's works are not just for adults but for everyone. By adapting these plays for children, I hope to plant the seeds of appreciation for classic literature in the fertile ground of young imaginations, encouraging a lifelong journey of reading, learning, and discovery.

I truly hope you will enjoy reading it, as much as I enjoyed re-writing it.

INTRODUCTION

Step into the vibrant and comedic world of "The Merry Wives of Windsor," where wit and cunning turn everyday life into an unforgettable adventure! Imagine a town where social status and the pursuit of love create a playground for mischief, all centered around one of Shakespeare's most beloved characters, Sir John Falstaff. This isn't just a story about romantic entanglements; it's a delightful exploration of humor, revenge, and the enduring charm of human folly.

Our tale unfolds in the charming town of Windsor, a place buzzing with the whispers of gossip and the schemes of those looking to outsmart one another. At the heart of this merry chaos is Falstaff, a knight with more appetite for pleasure and trickery than for honor or bravery. Despite his questionable morals and bumbling nature, Falstaff's wit and love for life make him an irresistible force, propelling him into the schemes of love and wealth.

INTRODUCTION

Falstaff devises a cunning plan to court two wealthy married women, Mistress Page and Mistress Ford, hoping to improve his financial standing. Little does he know, the merry wives are more than a match for him, leading to a series of comedic misunderstandings and misadventures. As Falstaff's plans unravel, Windsor's residents find themselves entangled in a web of deception, love triangles, and hilarious counterplots.

The story celebrates the cleverness of its women, who navigate the challenges and expectations of their society with humor and intelligence. It also touches on themes of jealousy, friendship, and the joy of life's unpredictabilities. Through clever disguises, secret messages, and a fair share of eavesdropping, "The Merry Wives of Windsor" delights in the triumph of wit over greed and the celebration of community spirit.

So, prepare to laugh and be charmed by the ingenious residents of Windsor. Journey through bustling streets, cozy homes, and the lush English countryside, all alive with the energy of clever plots and playful banter. Witness how Falstaff, with his grand plans and larger-than-life personality, becomes the unsuspecting hero of a story that celebrates the joy of life and the humor in humanity.

Are you ready? Let's dive into the joyful and mischievous world of "The Merry Wives of Windsor," where every jest is a lesson in wit and every folly is a cause for laughter. Join us on this heartwarming journey where we'll discover that in the game of love and mischief, it's not just about winning but about how much joy you can bring to the lives around you. This tale isn't just an escapade; it's a celebration of the vibrant tapestry of human relationships and the enduring power of laughter.

ACT 1

SCENE I

In the town of Windsor, right in front of Mr. Page's house, Mr. Shallow, Mr. Slender, and Sir Hugh Evans were having a chat.

Mr. Shallow was quite upset. "Sir Hugh, no matter what, I'm not letting this go. Even if there were twenty Sir John Falstaffs, he can't just treat me badly. I won't allow it."

Mr. Slender, trying to sound important, added, "In Gloucester, I'm known as a justice of peace, a big deal there."

"Yes, cousin Slender, a very big deal," Mr. Shallow agreed, nodding.

· · ·

"And not just any justice," Slender continued, puffing up a bit. "One with a fancy title, right, Mr. Parsons? It means I'm very important on official papers."

Mr. Shallow smiled, "Yes, that's right. And I've been important like this for a very long time."

"All the Shallows before me were just as grand, and all the Shallows after me will be too. We've got a tradition to uphold," Slender said proudly.

Mr. Shallow agreed, "It's a very old tradition."

Sir Hugh Evans, trying to lighten the mood, joked, "An old tradition that fits like an old coat, and it's all about love, isn't it?"

Mr. Shallow laughed, "Well, the fish on our coat, the luce, it's fresh. But an old coat, that's something different."

"I could add it to my own coat, right?" Slender asked, hopeful.

"You could, if you get married," Mr. Shallow teased.

. . .

"That would be a mess, wouldn't it?" Sir Hugh chuckled.

"Not at all," Mr. Shallow disagreed.

"But if he shares your coat, you'd have less of it for yourself," Sir Hugh pointed out, trying to explain his joke. "Anyway, if Sir John Falstaff has wronged you, I'm here to help make things right. I'll do my best to help you two sort it out."

Mr. Shallow was quite adamant, "This matter should go to the council; it's a big fuss."

Sir Hugh Evans tried to reason, "It's not good to bring a fuss to the council. They should hear about respect and good behavior, not about fights. Think carefully about this."

Mr. Shallow reminisced, "Ah, if I were younger, I'd settle this with a sword."

"But it's better to settle things as friends than with swords," Sir Hugh suggested, then added a new idea. "There's Miss Anne Page, the daughter of Mr. Thomas Page. She's a lovely young lady."

. . .

"Miss Anne Page? She has brown hair and speaks softly, like a lady should," Mr. Slender noted.

"Yes, exactly her! And she'll inherit a lot of money from her grandfather, over seven hundred pounds, when she turns seventeen. It might be a good idea to think about a marriage between you, Mr. Slender, and Miss Anne," Sir Hugh proposed.

"Her grandfather left her seven hundred pounds?" Slender asked, surprised.

"Yes, and her father will add more to that," Sir Hugh confirmed.

"I know her; she's very gifted," Slender noted, impressed.

"Seven hundred pounds and more to come are indeed great gifts," Sir Hugh agreed.

"Let's go visit Master Page. Is Falstaff there?" Mr. Shallow wondered aloud.

"Would I lie to you? I can't stand liars. Yes, Sir John is there. And I suggest we go with goodwill," Sir Hugh said as he knocked on Mr. Page's door, calling out, "Blessings to this house!"

· · ·

From inside, Mr. Page responded, "Who's there?"

As Mr. Page came out, Sir Hugh greeted him, "Blessings from God, your friend, and Justice Shallow. And here's young Mr. Slender, who might have an interesting proposal if you're inclined to hear it."

Mr. Page greeted them warmly, "I'm very happy to see you all well. Thank you for the venison, Mr. Shallow."

Mr. Shallow replied, "I'm also glad to see you, Mr. Page. I hope the venison was to your liking, though I wish it had been better prepared. How is Mrs. Page doing? I'm always grateful to you."

Mr. Page expressed his thanks, and Mr. Shallow reiterated his gratitude, emphasizing his sincerity.

Seeing Mr. Slender, Mr. Page said, "It's good to see you too, Mr. Slender."

Mr. Slender, curious, asked, "How's your greyhound doing? I heard he didn't do too well in a recent race."

Mr. Page was noncommittal, "It's hard to say for sure."

. . .

"You won't admit it, huh?" Slender teased.

Mr. Shallow chimed in, defending the dog, "It's a fine dog, no doubt about it."

Mr. Page, somewhat dismissive, labeled the dog as merely a mutt.

But Mr. Shallow insisted, "It's a good and fine dog. By the way, is Sir John Falstaff here?"

"Yes, he's here," Mr. Page confirmed, "and I wish I could help make things right between you two."

Sir Hugh Evans admired this approach, noting it was the Christian way to speak.

Mr. Shallow, feeling wronged, said, "Sir John has done me wrong."

Mr. Page agreed, "He somewhat admits to it."

Mr. Shallow argued, "But admitting it doesn't fix the wrong he's done to me."

. . .

Just then, Sir John Falstaff arrived with his friends, Bardolph, Nym, and Pistol.

Falstaff, with a hint of challenge, asked, "So, Mr. Shallow, are you going to complain about me to the king?"

Mr. Shallow didn't hesitate, "You've caused me trouble, Sir John. You've beaten up my workers, killed my deer, and broken into my property."

Sir John Falstaff, with a cheeky grin, added, "And what about your keeper's daughter? Did I not treat her kindly too?"

Mr. Shallow, not amused, brushed it off, "That's nothing! We will settle this matter properly."

Falstaff confidently admitted, "I'll answer for everything I've done. So, there you have it."

Mr. Shallow was firm, "The council will hear about your actions."

. . .

Falstaff laughed it off, "You'd actually be the one embarrassed if this went to council."

Sir Hugh Evans tried to calm things with a wise word, but Falstaff joked back about good plants, likening them to good stories.

Turning to Mr. Slender, Falstaff challenged, "I heard I broke your head. Do you have any grievances against me?"

Mr. Slender, annoyed, replied, "Yes, I do have issues with you and your tricky friends, Bardolph, Nym, and Pistol."

Bardolph insulted Slender, calling him a "Banbury cheese," to which Slender simply said it didn't matter.

Pistol and Nym added their jibes, but Slender ignored them, wondering aloud where his servant, Simple, had gone.

Sir Hugh Evans called for peace, explaining that they should solve this dispute calmly with three judges: Mr. Page, himself, and the innkeeper from the Garter Inn.

Mr. Page agreed, "We'll listen to the problem and resolve it together."

. . .

Sir Hugh Evans planned to note everything down for a careful discussion later.

Falstaff called out to Pistol, who responded with a nonsensical phrase, earning a scold from Sir Hugh for his silly talk.

Falstaff, with a serious tone, turned to Pistol, "Pistol, did you take Master Slender's money?"

Master Slender was upset, "Indeed, he did. I'd never step into my room again if not, with seven small coins and two special coins I bought, all gone!"

Falstaff questioned, "Is this true, Pistol?"

Sir Hugh Evans quickly said, "If it's stealing, then it's not true."

Pistol, feeling accused, retorted strongly, "You're wrong! Sir John, I swear, it wasn't me."

Slender insisted, pointing his finger, "He's the one, by these gloves!"

. . .

Nym tried to calm things down, "Let's not get heated. I'm telling you, it wasn't me."

But Slender wasn't convinced, "Well, someone took it when I was confused. I might have been tipsy, but I'm not foolish."

Falstaff looked around, "What do the rest of you say?"

Bardolph joked, "He was so out of it, he couldn't even speak properly."

Sir Hugh Evans corrected him, "You mean he lost his senses."

Bardolph laughed, "Exactly, he was beyond help then."

Slender, feeling a bit embarrassed but determined, declared, "Well, I'll only drink with good, honest folks from now on. No more tricks for me."

Sir Hugh Evans nodded approvingly, "That's a good decision, a very good decision indeed."

As the discussion about the missing purse and accusations continued, Anne Page arrived, carrying wine, followed by

Mistress Ford and Mistress Page. Mr. Page saw his daughter and suggested, "Dear, take the wine inside; we'll enjoy it there."

Slender's eyes lit up at the sight of Anne, "Oh wow! That's Miss Anne Page."

Mr. Page greeted Mistress Ford warmly, "How are you, Mistress Ford!"

Falstaff, ever the charmer, couldn't resist a moment, "Mistress Ford, what a pleasure to see you. May I?" he said, giving her a kiss on the cheek.

Mr. Page then turned to everyone, "Please, make yourselves at home. We've got a hot venison pie waiting. Let's eat and forget any upset feelings."

After everyone else had gone inside, Shallow, Slender, and Sir Hugh Evans stayed back. Slender, suddenly remembering something else, lamented, "I wish I had my Book of Songs and Sonnets with me. I'd rather have that than forty shillings right now."

Just then, Simple walked in, and Slender asked him, "Simple, where have you been? I needed you! Do you have the Book of Riddles with you?"

. . .

Simple replied, a bit confused, "Book of Riddles? Didn't you lend it to Alice Shortcake last Halloween?"

Mr. Shallow then tried to get Slender's attention, "Come on, cousin; we need to talk. Sir Hugh has something important to discuss with you. Do you get what I mean?"

Slender nodded, "Yes, sir, I'll be reasonable. If it makes sense, I'll do it."

"But really listen to me," Mr. Shallow stressed, hoping Slender would truly understand the importance of the conversation about to happen.

As the group noticed Anne Page carrying wine with Mrs. Ford and Mrs. Page following, Mr. Page cheerfully called out, "Ah, Anne, take the wine in; we'll enjoy it inside."

Slender's eyes lit up at the sight of Anne, whispering excitedly, "Oh, heaven! That's Miss Anne Page."

Mr. Page greeted his wife and her friend, "Hello, Mrs. Ford! And my dear, please welcome our guests. We have a hot venison pasty for dinner. Let's hope it brings us all closer together."

. . .

After Anne and the ladies headed inside, Slender, left outside with Shallow and Sir Hugh, suddenly missed his book of songs and sonnets. Just then, Simple walked up.

Slender asked, "Simple, where have you been? I've had to fend for myself! Do you have the Book of Riddles with you?"

Simple scratched his head, "The Book of Riddles? Didn't you lend it to Alice Shortcake last All-hallowmas?"

Shallow, trying to bring the conversation back to the matter at hand, nudged Slender, "Come on, let's focus. Sir Hugh has something important to discuss with you, something about Miss Anne."

Slender nodded, understanding the gravity of the conversation now steering towards marriage.

Sir Hugh, trying to clarify, said, "We're talking about a very special matter—your potential marriage to Miss Anne Page."

Slender, a bit overwhelmed, replied, "I'm willing to consider it if the terms are fair."

. . .

Sir Hugh pressed on, "But do you really like her? Can you imagine spending your life with her?"

Shallow added, "It's important, Slender. Can you truly love her?"

Slender, pondering the question, finally said, "I suppose, with time, any small spark could grow into something more. If marrying her is what you suggest, then I'm open to it, hoping love will follow with time and familiarity."

As Sir Hugh Evans and Mr. Shallow excused themselves to join the dinner, praising their plans and expressing their eagerness to partake in the grace, Slender hesitated, caught in a moment of bashfulness and uncertainty.

"Fair Mistress Anne," Mr. Shallow gallantly said, "I'd turn back the years for a chance with you."

Anne, with a smile, responded, "The table is set, and my father is looking forward to welcoming you all."

"I shall not keep him waiting," Mr. Shallow declared, moving to follow Anne's lead.

· · ·

"And I wouldn't miss it for the world," Sir Hugh added, echoing Mr. Shallow's sentiment.

Left alone with Anne, Slender awkwardly shuffled his feet. "Oh, no thank you, truly. I'm quite alright out here."

"But the dinner is waiting, and so is my father," Anne insisted, her voice gentle yet insistent.

Slender, trying to find any excuse, replied, "Really, I'm not hungry. But thank you for the kindness. Please, go ahead without me."

Anne, not willing to give up, pressed on, "We can't start without you. It wouldn't be right."

Slender, caught in a mix of shyness and politeness, finally conceded, albeit reluctantly, under Anne's persistent and gracious insistence. "Well, if you insist, I suppose I could join. But just for a bit."

Slender was trying his best to politely decline joining the dinner, explaining to Miss Anne that a recent injury and the smell of hot meat were putting him off. "I bumped my shin pretty badly the other day while practicing some sword fighting. Ever since then, hot food just doesn't sit well with me. And, oh, are those dogs barking at bears in town?" he asked, trying to change the subject.

Anne, playing along, mentioned, "I believe there might be bears, sir. I've heard people talking about them."

This piqued Slender's interest. "Oh, I enjoy bear-baiting quite a bit, though it often ends in quarrels. You don't like seeing bears loose, do you?" he inquired, trying to gauge her reaction.

"Yes, it frightens me," Anne admitted, showing a common fear of the time.

Slender shared a bit of his bravado, "Ah, but for me, that's the thrill of it! I've faced down a bear more than once. But I must say, the screams and fright of the ladies do tend to spoil the fun. Bears aren't exactly the most pleasant creatures, especially up close."

Just then, Mr. Page reappeared, urging Slender to join them for dinner, "Come along, Master Slender, we're all waiting on you."

"I really can't eat, but thank you," Slender repeated, trying to maintain his polite refusal.

· · ·

Mr. Page wouldn't hear of it, insisting, "You must join us, no excuses. Let's go."

Reluctantly, Slender agreed to follow, "Alright, but please, you go ahead."

"No, no, after you, Mistress Anne," he tried to defer to Anne, showing his manners.

Anne, however, insisted, "No, sir, you should lead."

Slender, ever the gentleman but not wanting to cause a scene, concluded, "I'd rather not impose any further. Please, let's not make this any more complicated." And with that, they all proceeded to the dining room, leaving the topic of bears and bruised shins behind.

SCENE 2

In the quiet streets, Sir Hugh Evans had a mission for Simple. "Off you go," he said with a firm but friendly voice, "and find Doctor Caius' house. Once you're there, look for Mistress Quickly. She takes care of many things in his house, like cooking and cleaning."

Simple nodded, "Alright, sir."

"But wait, there's something more important," Sir Hugh continued, pulling out a letter. "You must give this letter to Mistress Quickly. She knows Mistress Anne Page well, and this letter is asking for her help to win Mistress Anne's heart for your master. Please hurry and deliver it. And after you've done so, I can finish my lunch. There's still apples and cheese waiting for me."

. . .

With the letter in hand, Simple set off on his task, leaving Sir Hugh to look forward to his simple yet satisfying meal.

SCENE 3

In a room at the Garter Inn, Falstaff, a large and cheerful man, was with his friends: the Host of the inn, Bardolph, Nym, Pistol, and young Robin.

Falstaff called out, "Hey, innkeeper of the Garter!"

The Host replied with a smile, "What do you want, my good friend? Tell me wisely."

Falstaff sighed, "I have to let some of my helpers go."

"Don't worry, strong Falstaff; send them away. Let them find their own paths," the Host encouraged him.

. . .

21

Falstaff mentioned, "I have a budget of ten pounds a week."

The Host, impressed, said, "You're like a king, Falstaff! And for Bardolph, I'll give him a job. He can pour drinks for us. Right, big hero?"

"Sounds good to me," Falstaff agreed with a nod.

The Host then decided, "Bardolph, you'll work for us now, pouring drinks and taking care of the bar. Let's see how you do."

Once the Host left, Falstaff told Bardolph, "Follow him. Being a bartender is a good job. You can turn an old coat into a new vest; it's a fresh start for you. Goodbye."

Bardolph, excited, replied, "This is the job I've always wanted. I'm sure to do well."

Pistol, a bit rudely, teased Bardolph about his new job, "Oh, you think you can handle the tap, do you?"

Bardolph just left to follow the Host's orders, leaving his friends behind.

. . .

Nym chuckled, "He decided that after a few drinks, didn't he? Quite the funny decision."

Falstaff, glad to be moving on, said, "I'm happy to be rid of that trouble. He was too obvious with his sneaky ways, like a bad singer who can't keep the beat."

Nym thoughtfully added, "The real trick is to take what you can when nobody's looking."

Pistol, with a bit of flair, said, "The smart ones call it 'conveying.' To just say 'steal' is too crude!"

Falstaff, looking a bit troubled, confessed, "Friends, I'm nearly out of money."

Pistol joked, "Then, let your shoes wear out as well."

Falstaff, serious now, admitted, "There's no other way; I need to find a way to get by. I must be clever."

"Young birds need to eat," Pistol said, understandingly.

· · ·

Falstaff then asked, "Do any of you know Mr. Ford of this town?"

Pistol replied, "Yes, I know him. He's quite wealthy."

Falstaff shared his plan, "My dear friends, I'll tell you what I'm planning."

Pistol teased, "You mean, how wide you are?"

Ignoring the joke, Falstaff continued, "No jokes now, Pistol. Yes, I'm a big man, but I'm not talking about wasting. I'm talking about being smart with money. I plan to charm Mrs. Ford. She's friendly, she talks nicely, and she seems interested in me. I understand her hints, and they seem to say she likes me, Sir John Falstaff."

Pistol commented, "He has figured out what she wants and put it into simple words."

Nym asked, "Is that plan going to work?"

Falstaff explained, "Mrs. Ford controls her husband's money, and he has a lot of it."

. . .

Pistol encouraged him, "Then you should go for it."

Nym was amused, "This is getting interesting. Go on, tell us more about this plan."

Falstaff, smiling, said, "I've written her a letter, and one to Mrs. Page too. She also seemed quite interested in me, looking me over quite thoughtfully. Sometimes her glances made me feel quite special."

Falstaff and his friends were deep in a mischievous plot.

"Stealing at the right moment is the best kind of humor," Nym noted with a chuckle.

Pistol waved him off, saying, "The wise call it 'conveying'. 'Steal' is such a harsh word!"

Falstaff, rubbing his chin, admitted, "Friends, I'm nearly broke."

"So, let's make do with what we have," Pistol responded with a shrug.

. . .

Falstaff sighed, "I need to be clever to survive. I need to make some money."

"Young birds need to eat," Pistol agreed, nodding.

Falstaff then asked, "Who among you knows Ford, the man of this town?"

"I know him. He's rich," Pistol answered.

Falstaff leaned in, sharing his plan, "I've got an idea. I'm going to woo Ford's wife. She seems to like me."

Pistol laughed, "You've got her figured out!"

Nym asked, "Is this plan going to work?"

Falstaff smirked, "Ford's wife controls his money. She's my target."

Pistol encouraged him, "Then go for it, and we'll help."

· · ·

Falstaff revealed, "I've written letters to both Ford's wife and Page's wife. They both seem interested in me."

Pistol joked about Falstaff's confidence, "Like the sun shining on a rubbish heap."

Falstaff, undeterred, described how Ford's wife looked at him, "She checked me out so thoroughly, I felt like I was under a magnifying glass."

He continued, "I'm going to win them both over and make some money. Here, take these letters to Mrs. Page and Mrs. Ford."

As they prepared to leave, Falstaff gave Robin the letters, "Carry these carefully to the ladies."

Then, with a wave of his hand, he dismissed them, "Off you go, and let's see how this adventure unfolds."

Pistol and Nym left, plotting revenge and discussing how to expose Falstaff's plans to the husbands, Ford and Page. They were determined to stir up trouble.

SCENE 4

In Doctor Caius' house, Mistress Quickly was bustling about with energy. She spotted John Rugby and immediately asked for his help, "John Rugby, could you please peek outside and check if you see Master Doctor Caius coming? If he comes back and finds anyone here, oh, he won't be happy!"

Rugby nodded, "I'll go watch."

As Rugby left to look outside, Mistress Quickly shared a plan for later, "Let's have a warm drink by the fire tonight. It'll be cozy."

Rugby, she thought, was a good man - honest and hardworking. She mentioned to herself, "He's the best servant one could have, really. Just likes to pray a lot, but we all have our quirks."

Turning her attention to another visitor, she inquired, "Your name is Peter Simple, right?"

"Yes, that's me," Simple replied.

"And you work for Master Slender?" she continued.

"Yes, I do," Simple confirmed.

Mistress Quickly, curious about Master Slender, asked, "Does he have a big, round beard?"

"No, he has a small face and a light yellow beard," Simple corrected her.

"So, he's a gentle man, isn't he?" she deduced.

"Yes, very gentle. But don't let his looks fool you; he's quite strong and once even fought with a warrener," Simple shared, proud of his master.

· · ·

Mistress Quickly was surprised, "Really? He must be quite a character, walking with his head held high and strutting around!"

"Yes, that's exactly how he is," Simple agreed, nodding enthusiastically.

Mistress Quickly, now a bit worried, hoped for the best for Anne Page, a sweet girl they all cared about. "I'll talk to Parson Evans and see what I can do for your master. Anne is a lovely girl, and I hope--"

Suddenly, Rugby dashed back in, panic in his eyes, "Oh no! Here comes my master."

Mistress Quickly's heart raced. "Quick, hide in here!" she told Simple, pushing him into a closet to avoid being found by Doctor Caius. "Rugby, can you go check on my master? I'm worried something's wrong since he's not back yet," she added, trying to keep busy.

Just then, Doctor Caius stormed in, a frown on his face. "Why are you singing? I don't like these games. Get me the green box from my closet, do you understand? A green box."

. . .

"Right away, sir," Mistress Quickly said, relieved he hadn't decided to search the closet himself. "Thank goodness," she whispered to herself. "If he found the young man here, he'd be furious."

Doctor Caius, feeling hot and bothered, announced he was off to court for important business. "It's so hot... I must go to court —a big affair."

"Is this the box, sir?" Mistress Quickly held up the green box for him.

"Yes, put it in my pocket quickly. Where's that rascal Rugby?" Doctor Caius demanded.

"John Rugby! Where are you?" she called.

"Here, sir!" Rugby answered, appearing at once.

"You're John Rugby, and you'll come with me. Grab your sword, and let's head to the court," Doctor Caius commanded, setting off with urgency, leaving a trail of worry and relief behind him in his bustling house.

Rugby quickly told Doctor Caius, "It's ready, sir, right here."

. . .

Doctor Caius, realizing he was late, exclaimed, "Oh, I've spent too much time! Wait, I've forgotten something! There are some herbs in my closet I can't leave behind."

Mistress Quickly panicked, "Oh no, he's going to find the young man and be furious!"

As Doctor Caius rummaged through his closet, he discovered Simple hiding there. "What is this? A thief in my closet?" he yelled, pulling Simple out.

"Rugby, bring me my sword!" he demanded.

Mistress Quickly tried to calm him, "Please, sir, he's a good person."

"Why should a good person be in my closet? No one should be in there!" Doctor Caius was confused and angry.

Mistress Quickly pleaded, "Please listen. He came with a message from Parson Hugh."

Doctor Caius paused, "Alright, let's hear it."

. . .

Simple nervously said, "I was sent to ask your maid here to speak well of my master to Miss Anne Page, considering marriage."

Mistress Quickly interjected, "That's the whole story. But I'm staying out of this mess."

Doctor Caius, now a bit calmer, asked Rugby for some paper and began to write, pondering over the request.

Mistress Quickly, relieved at the calm, whispered to Simple, "I'm glad he's not more upset. I'll try to help your master as much as I can. My master, Doctor Caius, is quite fond of Miss Anne Page himself. But between us, I know Anne's true feelings, which is another matter entirely."

Simple, realizing the complexity of the situation, responded, "That sounds like a lot of responsibility."

Mistress Quickly agreed, "Yes, it's a lot to manage. But let's keep this between us. My master has his heart set on Miss Page, but her feelings are her own secret."

. . .

Doctor Caius was fuming with anger and had a plan in mind. "Take this letter to Sir Hugh," he instructed Simple sternly. "It's a challenge. I intend to confront him in the park for meddling in matters that don't concern him. Hurry now, don't stick around here."

Simple quickly left, understanding the seriousness of the situation.

Mistress Quickly tried to calm the air, "Oh, he's just speaking for his friend, that's all."

But Doctor Caius was determined, "Doesn't matter. Didn't you say Anne Page would be mine? I'll show that meddling priest. I've even arranged for a measurement of our weapons. Anne Page will be mine."

Trying to smooth things over, Mistress Quickly reassured him, "Sir, the young lady has a soft spot for you. Things will turn out fine. People will talk, but what does it matter?"

Doctor Caius wasn't pacified and made his intentions clear, "Rugby, we're off to the court. Mark my words, if I don't marry Anne Page, you're out of a job. Follow me."

. . .

As they left, Mistress Quickly muttered to herself, confident in her knowledge of Anne's true feelings, "He's dreaming if he thinks he has a chance with Anne. I know her heart better than anyone in Windsor."

Just then, Fenton called out from outside, curious about Anne.

Mistress Quickly greeted him warmly, "Good day, sir! What brings you here?"

Fenton was anxious for news about Anne, "How is she? Do you think I stand a chance with her?"

Mistress Quickly, always one to know the goings-on, assured him, "Trust me, she has a fondness for you. And that wart above your eye? We spent an hour talking about it. She's a special girl, though a bit prone to sadness at times. But for you, there's hope."

Fenton, eager and hopeful, made plans to see Anne Page that very day. "Here's some money for you," he said to Mistress Quickly, offering a coin. "Please, say good things about me to her if you see her before I do."

· · ·

"Oh, absolutely, I'll sing your praises!" Mistress Quickly promised with a smile. "And next time, we'll chat more about that wart of yours and all the others trying to win her over."

Fenton nodded, his mind already racing ahead to his meeting with Anne. "I must hurry now. Goodbye!" he said, rushing off.

"Goodbye, sir," Mistress Quickly called after him, watching as he disappeared. She mused to herself, "He's a true gentleman, but Anne's heart isn't set on him. I know what she's thinking better than anyone."

Then, a thought struck her, causing a moment of panic. "Oh, what have I forgotten now?" she wondered aloud, retracing her steps as she exited, her mind a whirl of tasks and secrets in the bustling world of Windsor.

ACT II

SCENE I

In front of Page's house, Mistress Page stood holding a letter with a puzzled look on her face.

"Oh, so now I get love letters? And at this age?" she wondered aloud. Curiosity got the better of her, and she started to read the letter. "It says, 'Don't ask me why I love you. Love doesn't always listen to reason. We're both not young, we both like to laugh, and we both enjoy a good drink. Isn't that enough to be happy about? I hope you can be happy with a soldier's love because I truly love you. I won't ask you to feel sorry for me; that's not how a soldier talks. Instead, I'll just say, love me. Yours truly, ready to fight for you any time, John Falstaff.'"

Mistress Page couldn't help but laugh. "What a strange man! He's old and yet tries to act like a young lover. How dare he be so bold when he barely knows me? This is too funny. I hardly showed him any attention. Oh, I have an idea. I'll make a joke out of this in the parliament, saying we should ban such men. But how will I get back at him? Oh, I'll find a way, as sure as the sky is blue."

Just then, Mistress Ford came by. "Mistress Page! I was just on my way to see you," she said with a smile.

"And I was about to visit you! You don't look well, though," Mistress Page observed.

Mistress Ford waved off the concern. "Oh, don't worry about me. I'm fine, really."

"But you do look a bit under the weather," Mistress Page insisted, still concerned but with a hint of a smile, knowing they both had much to talk about, especially about unexpected letters.

Mistress Ford looked a bit troubled but intrigued. "I feel a bit off, but I think you can help me with something bigger. Oh, Mistress Page, I need your advice!"

"What's bothering you?" Mistress Page asked, eager to help her friend.

. . .

Mistress Ford hesitated for a moment, then burst out, "Imagine, I could have been offered a great honor, if not for a tiny issue!"

"Forget the small stuff! Tell me about this honor," Mistress Page encouraged her.

"Well, it's a bit silly, but I could have been considered for a knighthood!" Mistress Ford said, half-jokingly.

"A knighthood? You're pulling my leg! Lady Alice Ford, huh?" Mistress Page laughed, playing along. "But knights are often not what they seem. Tell me more!"

"We're wasting the day. Here, read this letter. It's about how I could 'become a knight'," said Mistress Ford, passing a letter similar to the one Mistress Page had. "This letter made me laugh and frown at the same time. The man who wrote this praises modesty and scolds rudeness so well, you'd think he means every word. But his actions and words match as well as a folk song to a solemn hymn. What brought this man to our town? How should I deal with him? Maybe I should lead him on until his own foolish desires ruin him. Have you heard anything so odd?"

. . .

Mistress Page, holding her own letter, couldn't believe it. "This is almost the same as your letter, except for our names! It seems we're not the only ones he's trying to woo with his words. I bet he has a stack of these letters, just changing the names as needed. He doesn't care about the truth, only about wooing us. I'd rather face a giant than deal with his nonsense. But don't worry, we'll find a way to outsmart him, and we'll have a good laugh doing it!"

Mistress Ford was astounded. "It's the exact same! The handwriting, the words. What does he think of us?"

Mistress Page shook her head. "I'm not sure, but it's making me question my own self-respect. I'll pretend to be someone I'm not because, honestly, he must see something in me that I don't see myself for him to approach me like this."

Mistress Ford was determined. "Approach? Let's make sure we keep him in his place."

"And I'll do the same. If he tries anything, I'll never deal with him again. Let's plan a trick on him. We'll pretend to be interested, lead him on, until he's spent all his money chasing after us."

. . .

Mistress Ford agreed, "I'm in, as long as it doesn't make us look bad. Oh, if only my husband could see this letter. It would drive him crazy with jealousy."

Just then, their husbands approached. Mistress Page noted, "Here comes my husband, and yours too. He's not the jealous type, thankfully."

Mistress Ford sighed, "You're lucky."

"Let's work together to outsmart this cheeky knight," Mistress Page whispered as they moved aside to plot.

As they were plotting, Ford walked in with his friends, worried about rumors concerning his wife.

Pistol, one of Ford's friends, hinted, "Sir John has an eye on your wife."

Ford was puzzled. "But my wife isn't young."

Pistol explained, "He's not picky. He chases everyone, rich or poor, young or old. He loves the variety, Ford. Think about it."

· · ·

Mistress Ford and Mistress Page were whispering about the same curious letter they both received from Sir John Falstaff, wondering what he was thinking to send them such notes.

"I just can't figure it out," Mistress Page shook her head. "It's like he sees something in me that even I don't see. Why else would he send such a bold letter?"

Mistress Ford agreed, "It's so cheeky! But I have a plan. We'll pretend to go along with it, lead him on, and then play a trick on him that he'll never forget!"

Mistress Page laughed, "Yes, let's have some fun at his expense. We'll make him think he's winning our hearts and then pull the rug out from under him!"

As they were plotting their revenge, their husbands, Ford and Page, along with Pistol and Nym, appeared. Pistol, in a serious tone, warned Ford, "Sir John has his eyes on your wife. Be careful, or you might end up like Actaeon, chased by his own dogs."

Ford was taken aback, "My wife? But she's not even his type!"

Pistol ominously added, "He's not picky. He likes everyone. Watch out before it's too late." And with that, he left.

. . .

Ford was worried but determined to uncover the truth. Nym, speaking to Page, confirmed the bad news, "Falstaff is after your wife too. It's the honest truth. I'm not a fan of gossip, but you should know."

After Nym and Pistol left, Ford declared, "I'm going to find out what Falstaff is up to with my own eyes."

Page, however, wasn't convinced by the warnings. "Such a strange fellow. I can't take him seriously."

But Ford was already making plans. "I need to see this through."

Just then, Mistress Page and Mistress Ford came over. "Where are you off to, George?" asked Mistress Page, pretending not to know about the mischief afoot.

Together, they all stood, entangled in a web of misunderstandings and schemes, with each person unaware of the others' plans.

Mistress Ford greeted her husband with a smile, "Hello, dear Frank! You seem so quiet today. What's bothering you?"

. . .

Frank, surprised, replied, "Me, bothered? Oh, not at all. You should head back home."

"But you seem so lost in thought," Mistress Ford insisted, her curiosity piqued. Turning to her friend, Mistress Page, she suggested, "Shall we go, dear?"

Mistress Page agreed, "Let's. George, you'll join us for dinner, won't you?"

In a whisper, Mistress Ford and Mistress Page noticed someone approaching and thought of a plan. "Look, here comes the perfect person to send to that silly knight," whispered Mistress Ford.

Mistress Page nodded, whispering back, "Yes, I was thinking the same. She's the one for the job."

Just then, Mistress Quickly arrived, and Mistress Page asked her, "You're here to see my daughter Anne, aren't you?"

"Yes, indeed. And how is dear Anne doing?" asked Mistress Quickly, eager to know.

. . .

"Come with us. We have quite a bit to talk about," Mistress Page invited, and they all went inside together.

Outside, Master Ford ran into his friend, Page. "Did you hear what that fellow told me?" Ford asked, a bit troubled.

Page replied, "Yes, and did you hear what the other guy said to me?"

Ford wondered if there was any truth to the rumors, "Do you believe them?"

Page scoffed, "Those troublemakers? I doubt the knight would dare, but those accusing him are just bitter because they're out of a job now."

"Were they really his men?" Ford asked, seeking confirmation.

"Indeed, they were," Page admitted.

Ford frowned, "That doesn't make me feel any better. Is he staying at the Garter Inn?"

. . .

"Yes, he is. And if he dares try anything with my wife, I'll let her deal with him. She'll give him nothing but sharp words," Page declared, showing confidence in his wife's ability to handle the situation.

In the bustling streets near the Garter Inn, Master Ford confided in his friend, Page, "I trust my wife, truly, but it's hard not to worry. A man can never be too sure, and I'd rather not have any regrets."

Page pointed out cheerfully, "Look, here comes our lively host from the Garter Inn. He's either had a good drink or found some coin, judging by his bright mood."

As the Host approached, beaming, he greeted them, "Hello, my fine fellows! What brings you gentlemen here today?"

Following closely was Shallow, who joined in, "Good evening to you both! There's an exciting event planned. Care to join us?"

The Host, with a twinkle in his eye, hinted at the adventure, "Indeed, we've got a duel on our hands – between Sir Hugh, the Welsh priest, and Dr. Caius, the French doctor."

Ford, curious, pulled the Host aside for a private word, "Might I have a moment? There's something I need to discuss."

. . .

On the side, Shallow excitedly told Page about the duel, "It's going to be quite the spectacle. Our Host has even measured their weapons. I assure you, it's not to be missed."

Meanwhile, Ford made a peculiar request to the Host, "I've got no quarrel with your knightly guest, but I'd be grateful if you could introduce me to him as 'Brook' just for a bit of fun."

The Host agreed, delighted by the plan, "Of course, my friend! You'll have your meeting, and your secret's safe with me."

As they all prepared to leave for the duel, Page remarked, "I've heard the Frenchman is quite skilled with his rapier."

Shallow boasted of days past, "Ah, skill is one thing, but true courage comes from the heart. I remember when a sword in my hand meant something."

The Host rallied the group, "Come on, then! Let's not miss out on the fun."

As they departed, Ford stayed behind, lost in thought, "Page might trust his wife completely, but I have my doubts. I need to know for sure. I'll disguise myself and test Falstaff. If my wife proves faithful, then all is well. But if not, it's better to know the truth." With a plan in mind, Ford set off to unravel the mystery.

SCENE 2

In a cozy room of the Garter Inn, Falstaff was having a bit of a disagreement with his friend Pistol.

Falstaff, with a firm tone, said, "I won't give you any money."

Pistol, trying to be clever, replied, "Then, the world is my oyster, which I'll open with my sword."

But Falstaff wasn't convinced. "Not a penny from me. Look, I've been nice enough, letting you use my name to get out of trouble. I've asked my friends to help you out not once, but three times! If it weren't for that, you'd be in a real pickle. And I even vouched for you, saying you were brave and strong. And remember when Mistress Bridget's fan broke? I swore it wasn't you who took it."

Pistol, feeling a bit cornered, asked, "Didn't you get a share? Didn't you get some money from that?"

Falstaff shook his head. "Why should I risk my neck for nothing? Listen, don't hang around me anymore. I'm not here to save you. Go on, get out of here. And you think you're so honorable? I've bent over backwards trying to maintain my honor, even when it was really hard. And yet, you think you can just pretend to be honorable with your shabby clothes and big words? Not happening."

Pistol, seeing no way out, sighed, "Alright, I give up. What more do you want from a man?"

Just then, Robin, a young boy, came in with a message. "Sir, there's a lady who wants to talk to you."

"Let her come in," Falstaff said, curious.

A woman named Mistress Quickly entered the room with a bright smile. "Good morning to you, sir."

. . .

"Good morning, good lady," Falstaff greeted her back, wondering what she wanted.

Mistress Quickly seemed to hesitate at first, but then, gaining confidence, she began to speak more openly to Falstaff. "Not exactly, if it pleases you, sir."

Falstaff, intrigued, responded, "Oh, then you're a good lady."

"I promise, as true as the fact that I was born to my mother," she assured him earnestly.

"I believe you," Falstaff nodded, curious about what she had to say. "What's on your mind?"

"Could I share a word or two with you, sir?" Mistress Quickly asked tentatively.

"You can share two thousand if you'd like, and I'll listen," Falstaff offered generously.

"It's about Mistress Ford," she started, and then whispered, "Could you come a bit closer? I work for Doctor Caius."

. . .

"Yes, go on about Mistress Ford," urged Falstaff, leaning in.

"You're very right, sir. Please, just a little closer," she persisted.

"Don't worry, no one else can hear us. Only my people are here," Falstaff assured her.

"Is that so? May God bless them and keep them," Mistress Quickly said with a hint of relief.

"So, what about Mistress Ford?" Falstaff prompted again, eager to hear more.

"Oh, sir, she's a kind soul. But goodness, you're quite the charmer, aren't you? May heaven forgive us all," she chuckled, half-teasing, half-serious.

"Mistress Ford, let's focus on her," Falstaff urged, wanting to get to the heart of the matter.

Mistress Quickly got to the point, "Well, it's like this: you've made her the talk of the town, more than any nobleman or knight ever could. Even when the royal court was nearby, no one could get her attention like you have. There have been lords, knights, and gentlemen, all trying with letters and gifts, sweet scents and fancy clothes, speaking so nicely, and offering the finest wines and sweets. But none of them could win her over, not even for a moment. This morning, someone gave me twenty gold coins, but I stand by honesty above all. And despite all their attempts, not one of them could even get her to share a drink. Even earls, and more impressively, pensioners, tried their luck, but she treated them all the same."

Falstaff was eager to get to the point. "But what does she say about me? Keep it short, please."

Mistress Quickly was ready with her news. "She got your letter and thanks you so much. She wanted me to tell you that her husband will be away from home between ten and eleven."

"Ten and eleven?" Falstaff repeated, making a mental note.

"Yes, indeed. That's when you can visit, to see the... uh, picture she mentioned. Her husband, Master Ford, won't be around. Poor thing, she doesn't have it easy with him; he's very jealous, and she's not happy," Mistress Quickly shared sympathetically.

"Ten and eleven. Tell her I'll be there; I won't let her down," Falstaff promised.

. . .

"That's the spirit! Oh, and there's a message from Mistress Page too. She sends her best wishes and hints that her husband is often away. She thinks very highly of you. Both ladies seem quite taken with you!" Mistress Quickly teased.

Falstaff shrugged it off modestly. "Oh, it's nothing special about me. Just being myself, I guess."

Mistress Quickly smiled warmly at him. "You're too modest!"

Falstaff, curious, asked, "Have Mistress Ford and Mistress Page told each other about their... feelings for me?"

"Oh no, they wouldn't do that. But Mistress Page asked for a small favor – she wants you to send your little page to her. Her husband likes the lad, and it seems Master Page is a good man. Mistress Page leads a good life, gets to do as she pleases, and she truly deserves it. So, you'll need to send your page over to her," Mistress Quickly explained.

Falstaff agreed with a nod, "Of course, I will."

Mistress Quickly advised, "Please do, and have the boy carry messages between you both. Make sure to have a secret word so you can communicate without him understanding. It's not good for children to know about adult matters."

. . .

With a smile, Falstaff said, "Take care. Say hello to them for me. Here's some money for your trouble. And boy, follow this lady." Mistress Quickly and the boy, Robin, then left.

Falstaff was left pondering the situation when Pistol chimed in with encouragement, likening Mistress Quickly to a messenger of love and urging Falstaff to pursue his prize.

"Alright, off you go, Pistol. Maybe there's more for you in this adventure than before," Falstaff mused, contemplating the turn of events.

Just then, Bardolph entered with news of a visitor named Master Brook, who wished to meet Falstaff and had sent a gift of wine.

"Brook, you say?" Falstaff perked up, interested.

"Yes, sir," Bardolph confirmed before going to invite the visitor in.

Falstaff was amused, "Ah, guests bearing gifts are always welcome, especially when it's wine. Ah, Mistress Ford and Mistress Page, what a web we weave!"

. . .

Bardolph returned with Ford, who was disguised and introduced himself as Brook.

"Bless you, sir!" Ford greeted.

"And you! What can I do for you?" Falstaff inquired, curious about his new guest.

Ford, trying to seem casual, replied, "I hope I'm not being too forward. I've come to seek your acquaintance."

"Welcome, Master Brook. I'm keen to know you better," Falstaff responded, intrigued by the visit.

Ford, looking a bit troubled, turned to Falstaff and said, "Sir John, I come to you not asking for money, but to share a burden I carry. You see, I have too much money and it's a hassle. Could you help me by taking some?"

Falstaff, surprised, replied, "I'm not sure how carrying your money would suit me, but I'm listening."

. . .

Ford, eager to explain, continued, "Well, Sir John, I've known of you for a long time and admired you from a distance. I have something personal to share, and I hope you'll bear with me."

"Go on," Falstaff encouraged him.

"There's a woman in this town, married to a man named Ford," Ford started, hesitantly.

"Yes, continue," Falstaff said, nodding.

Ford sighed deeply. "I've loved her for a long time, Sir John. I've spent a fortune trying to win her heart. I've followed her, showered her with gifts, and even paid others just to see her or to find out what she might like."

Falstaff listened intently as Ford poured out his heart, speaking of his unrequited love and the lengths he had gone to for a glimpse of affection from her. Ford concluded with a heavy heart, "But all my efforts have been in vain, Sir John. It feels like chasing a shadow, always out of reach. Love, it seems, runs away when you chase it too desperately."

Falstaff, curious, asked, "So, she never gave you any hope or promise?"

· · ·

Ford shook his head. "No, never."

"And you never asked her directly about your feelings?" Falstaff pressed on.

Again, Ford answered, "No, never."

Falstaff pondered, "Then, how would you describe your love?"

Ford sighed, "Like building a beautiful house on someone else's land. I lost everything because I built it in the wrong place."

"Why are you telling me all this?" Falstaff wondered.

Ford leaned in, "This is my whole point. Some say she acts differently when she's away from me, more free. You, Sir John, are a man of the world, skilled in conversation and respected by many. I have money. I'm willing to spend it all if you help me. Try to win over Ford's wife, use your charm, convince her."

Falstaff raised an eyebrow, "Do you think it's right for me to win her over for you to enjoy? That seems backward to me."

. . .

Ford explained, "I just want to prove something. She's so sure of her honor that I can't even approach her. If I could show that she's not as perfect as she seems, maybe I'd have a chance. What do you think?"

Falstaff was caught in the intricacies of Ford's plan, seeing both the challenge and the opportunity it presented.

Falstaff confidently accepted Ford's proposal, starting with a bold claim, "Master Brook, I'll gladly take your money. Give me your hand, and I promise you, as a gentleman, you'll get what you wish for with Ford's wife."

Ford was overwhelmed with gratitude. "Oh, thank you, sir!"

Falstaff assured him further, "You won't need to worry about money or Mistress Ford; you'll lack for nothing. I'm already set to meet her at her own request. Her husband will be out, and that's when I'll see her. Come see me tonight, and I'll tell you how it went."

Ford expressed his happiness at meeting Falstaff, then tried to warn him about Mr. Ford, suggesting it might be best to avoid him if possible.

. . .

Falstaff scoffed at the idea of fearing Ford, calling him a fool and vowing to outsmart him. "I'll handle him. And you, Master Brook, will see how I deal with such a peasant and win over his wife. Meet me tonight."

After Falstaff left, Ford was left alone, wrestling with his emotions and the complexity of his plan. He berated himself for the jealousy that led him to this point, yet he was determined to catch his wife in the act, expose Falstaff's intentions, and save his honor. He resolved to act quickly, lamenting the bitter title of being a cuckold and vowing to prevent his wife's betrayal, exact revenge on Falstaff, and make a fool of Page for his trustful nature. Ford's heart was heavy with suspicion and the desire for retribution as he set out to foil the plans and safeguard his dignity.

SCENE 3

In a field near Windsor, Doctor Caius and his helper, Rugby, were waiting for someone. Doctor Caius, who was a bit impatient, called out, "Jack Rugby!"

Rugby quickly replied, "Yes, sir?"

"What time is it, Jack?" Doctor Caius asked.

Rugby answered, "It's later than the time Sir Hugh promised to meet us, sir."

Doctor Caius was a bit relieved and annoyed at the same time. "Oh, he's saved himself by not coming. He must have prayed really hard to avoid meeting me because if he had shown up, it would have been bad news for him."

Rugby tried to explain, "Sir Hugh is smart. He knew you might get really mad at him if he came."

But Doctor Caius was feeling bold. "Oh, I'll make sure he regrets it if he ever shows up. Get your sword, Jack; I'll show you how I plan to confront him."

Poor Rugby was worried. "Oh dear, sir, I don't know how to fight."

Doctor Caius insisted, "Come on, take your sword."

Just then, they were interrupted by the arrival of a few guests: the Host, Shallow, Slender, and Page. They all greeted Doctor Caius warmly.

"What brings all of you here?" Doctor Caius asked, curious and a bit annoyed.

The Host was eager and a bit cheeky. "We're here to see you fight, to watch your skillful moves and see you in action!"

· · ·

Doctor Caius scoffed at the idea of fighting the person they were expecting. "Oh, that coward? The priest? He wouldn't dare show his face here."

The field near Windsor was filled with anticipation, but also a bit of humor as they all waited to see what would happen next.

The Host teased Doctor Caius, "You're like a mighty warrior, a real Hector of Greece, my boy!"

Doctor Caius was eager to make his point, "Please, everyone, remember I waited here for hours for him, and he never showed up."

Shallow tried to offer some wisdom, "Master Doctor, maybe it's for the best. He looks after souls, and you look after bodies. Fighting doesn't suit either of your jobs, does it, Master Page?"

Page chimed in with a chuckle, "Master Shallow, you were quite the fighter yourself, though now you're a man of peace."

Shallow, with a twinkle in his eye, replied, "Ah, but even though I seek peace now, the sight of a sword still tempts me to action. We may grow older and wiser, but the spark of youth never fully leaves us, right, Master Page?"

. . .

Page nodded, "That's very true, Master Shallow."

Shallow then turned to Doctor Caius, "Master Doctor, I'm here to take you back home. You've shown great wisdom today, as has Sir Hugh. It's time to leave this place."

But the Host wanted to stir things up a bit more, "Just a moment, Monsieur Mockwater."

Doctor Caius was confused, "Mock-water? What's that?"

The Host teased, "In our language, it means courage, my dear doctor."

Doctor Caius, not wanting to be outdone, boasted, "Well, then, I have as much courage as any Englishman. That cowardly priest, I swear I'll teach him a lesson!"

The Host laughed, "He might just fight back hard, my friend."

Doctor Caius, puzzled again, asked, "Fight back? What do you mean?"

. . .

The Host explained, "It means he might just make up for all this trouble."

Doctor Caius, determined, declared, "Well, he better make it up to me, because I won't let this go."

The Host playfully concluded, "And I'll make sure he gets the message, or my name isn't the Host!"

Doctor Caius warmly thanked the Host for his help. The Host, looking to stir up a little adventure, suggested, "But first, let's have Master Page, and our friends go through the town to Frogmore."

Page, catching on, whispered, "Sir Hugh is there, isn't he?"

The Host confirmed with a sly smile, "Yes, he's there. Let's see how he's feeling, and I'll take the doctor here on a little detour through the fields. Sound good?"

Shallow agreed, "We'll do it."

Page, Shallow, and Slender all bid Doctor Caius farewell for now and left.

. . .

Doctor Caius, still a bit fired up, declared, "I swear, I'm going to get that priest; he's caused enough trouble."

The Host tried to calm him down, "Let's not rush to anger. Instead, let's take a walk through the fields to Frogmore. I'll take you to where Mistress Anne Page is having a feast at a farmhouse. You can try to win her heart there. How does that sound?"

Doctor Caius, now intrigued by the plan, thanked the Host, "Oh, thank you! I like this plan. And I'll make sure you meet some of my important friends and patients as a thank you."

The Host, playing along, added, "And I'll help you with Anne Page. Do we have a deal?"

Doctor Caius was pleased, "Yes, that sounds perfect."

With their plan set, the Host encouraged, "Let's go, then."

Doctor Caius called for Rugby to follow, "Come on, Jack Rugby. Let's not dawdle."

And with that, they all set off for their next adventure.

ACT III

SCENE I

In a green field near Frogmore, Sir Hugh Evans stood with Simple, who worked for Master Slender. Sir Hugh was on a mission and looked quite serious.

"Simple, my good fellow," Sir Hugh started, "have you seen Doctor Caius around? He claims to be a doctor."

"Oh yes, Sir Hugh, I've looked here and there, up and down, every direction but the town's heart," Simple replied with a bit of a confused look.

"Then, please, could you also check the town way?" Sir Hugh asked, almost pleading.

· · ·

"Right away, sir!" Simple said, ready to dash off again.

Left alone, Sir Hugh couldn't help but talk to himself. "Oh dear, my heart's racing, and I'm all over the place! I almost wish Dr. Caius has tricked me. How upset I am! If I get the chance, I'll give him a piece of my mind," he muttered, trying to shake off his nerves.

To calm himself, Sir Hugh started singing softly about beautiful rivers and singing birds, but his emotions got the better of him, and he felt tears coming.

Just then, Simple hurried back. "Sir, sir, Dr. Caius is coming this way!"

Sir Hugh brightened a bit. "Ah, let him come. Maybe singing will help," he thought and continued his song, hoping to ease his worry.

"What's he carrying? Any weapons?" Sir Hugh asked suddenly, a bit anxious.

"No weapons, sir. It's just him and Master Shallow, coming over from Frogmore," Simple assured him, pointing in their direction.

· · ·

In the chilly morning air, Sir Hugh Evans was getting a bit flustered and asked for his gown to be brought to him. Just then, Page, Shallow, and Slender walked up, greeting him cheerfully.

"Good morning, Sir Hugh! How do you do on this fine day?" Shallow exclaimed, always happy to see his friend.

Slender, spotting someone he had a crush on, whispered to himself dreamily, "Ah, sweet Anne Page!"

Page chimed in with a warm, "Hello, Sir Hugh! How are you?"

Sir Hugh, ever the kind soul, blessed them, "May you all be protected and happy!"

Shallow, with a twinkle in his eye, teased Sir Hugh about balancing his religious duties with his love for learning, "Are you juggling both the sword of faith and the word of knowledge, Sir Hugh?"

Page couldn't help but comment on Sir Hugh's outfit, "Still dressed so young in this cold, aren't you, Sir Hugh?"

. . .

Sir Hugh, a bit defensively, replied, "There's a good reason for it."

"We've come to ask for your help with something important," Page mentioned, hinting at a serious matter.

Sir Hugh was intrigued, "Oh? What's that?"

Page explained there was a very upset gentleman nearby, "He's really worked up because he feels someone has wronged him. I've never seen anyone so out of sorts."

Shallow added, "In all my long years, I've never seen a man of his wisdom so upset."

Curious, Sir Hugh asked, "Who is this man?"

Page answered, "I think you know him. It's Master Doctor Caius, the French doctor."

This news didn't please Sir Hugh at all. "Oh, him? I'd rather you talk about anything else. He might know a lot about medicine, but he's not a good man, and he's quite a coward too."

. . .

Sir Hugh Evans, feeling a bit chilly, asked for his gown to be brought to him or at least held by someone nearby. Just then, Page, Shallow, and Slender walked over to greet him warmly.

"Good morning, Sir Hugh! It's quite something to keep a gamer away from his dice and a student from his books, isn't it?" Shallow joked, smiling.

Slender, lost in his thoughts, quietly sighed, "Ah, sweet Anne Page."

Page chimed in with a cheerful, "Hello, good Sir Hugh!"

"Bless you all, for your own good," Sir Hugh replied, giving them a nod.

Shallow, always looking for a bit of humor, teased, "What's this? The sword and the Bible? Do you practice both, master parson?"

Page couldn't help but comment on Sir Hugh's attire, "And still in your doublet and hose on such a cold, damp day!"

Sir Hugh, a bit embarrassed, simply said, "There's a reason for everything."

. . .

Page then got straight to the point. "We've come to seek your help, master parson."

"Oh? What for?" Sir Hugh inquired, curious.

"It's about a very respected gentleman who seems to have been wronged. He's quite upset, more than I've ever seen," Page explained.

Shallow, nodding, added, "In all my years, I've never seen someone of his knowledge and position so disturbed."

"And who might this be?" Sir Hugh wondered aloud.

"You know him; it's Master Doctor Caius, the famous French doctor," Page revealed.

Sir Hugh couldn't hide his disdain. "God's will! I'd rather hear about a bowl of porridge than him."

"Why so?" Page asked, puzzled by the reaction.

. . .

"Because he knows nothing about medicine, and he's a coward too," Sir Hugh declared firmly.

Just as they were discussing, Page hinted that Doctor Caius was ready for a duel. Shallow, still daydreaming about Anne, agreed, noting that Caius's readiness could be seen in his choice of weapons. They all urged for caution as Doctor Caius approached with Rugby and the Host.

"Please, master parson, let's not resort to violence," Page advised.

"And you too, Doctor, please," Shallow added, hoping to prevent any trouble.

The Host suggested a peaceful resolution. "Let's have them talk it out and keep it friendly, without anyone getting hurt," he said.

Doctor Caius, frustrated, approached Sir Hugh. "Why didn't you meet me as promised?" he demanded.

Sir Hugh, trying to keep the peace, whispered, "Let's be patient, everything in good time."

· · ·

But Doctor Caius was angry, calling Sir Hugh a coward directly.

Sir Hugh, still hoping to avoid a public scene, whispered back, suggesting they find a peaceful solution. But publicly, he stood his ground, accusing Doctor Caius of avoiding their duel.

Doctor Caius was incredulous, insisting he had been waiting to confront Sir Hugh as agreed. Sir Hugh suggested they let the Host of the Garter make the final judgement on their dispute.

The Host stepped in, trying to calm everyone down. "Let's have peace, between the French and the Welsh, between the healer of souls and the healer of bodies!"

Doctor Caius, liking the sound of that, agreed, "Ah, that's good; excellent."

"Listen to me, the host of the Garter Inn. Am I smart? Am I clever? Do I think like a strategist? Should I lose my doctor? No, he's the one who gives me medicines and treatments. Should I lose my priest, my Sir Hugh? No, he's the one who gives me wise sayings. Let's shake hands, both of you," the Host said, trying to bridge the gap between the two. "I've tricked you both, sending you on a wild goose chase. Your hearts are strong, and you're not hurt. Let's forget this fight and have a drink instead. Come, let's put down our swords and follow me."

. . .

Shallow laughed, "What a crazy host! Let's follow him, gentlemen."

Slender, still daydreaming about Anne, quietly sighed her name as they all followed the Host out.

Left alone, Doctor Caius couldn't help but laugh a little, "Did he trick us? Made fools of us, ha?"

Sir Hugh, now seeing the humor in the situation, suggested, "He's made us look silly, but let's be friends and think of a way to get back at him, this tricky host."

"By all means, I agree," said Doctor Caius, shaking hands with Sir Hugh. "He promised to help me meet Anne Page but tricked me too."

"Well, then, let's team up and teach him a lesson," Sir Hugh proposed, eager to plan their revenge.

And with that, they left together, plotting their next move.

SCENE 2

In a sunny street, Mistress Page was walking with a young boy named Robin. She teased him a bit, saying, "You used to follow everyone around, but look at you now, leading the way! Would you rather be showing me the way or running after your master?"

Robin, with a spark in his eye, replied, "I'd much rather walk in front of you than trail behind him."

Mistress Page laughed. "Oh, what a charmer you are! You'll surely grow up to be quite the smooth talker."

Just then, Mr. Ford came along and greeted Mistress Page, "Hello, Mistress Page! Where are you off to?"

. . .

She smiled, "Oh, just off to visit your wife. Is she home?"

"Yes, she's there. She's quite bored, I'd guess, lacking company," Ford replied, a bit cheekily adding, "I think if your husbands were out of the picture, you and she might just end up marrying each other!"

Mistress Page chuckled, "Well, if that were the case, we'd find two new husbands!"

Ford noticed Robin and asked, "And who is this young fellow?"

Mistress Page replied, still amused, "Oh, this little mystery? My husband brought him home, but for the life of me, I can never remember his name. What did you say your name was, young sir?"

With a little bow, Robin answered, "Sir John Falstaff, sir."

"Sir John Falstaff!" Ford exclaimed, surprised.

"Yes, that's the one! I always forget," Mistress Page laughed. "There's such a friendship between him and my husband. So, your wife is really at home, then?"

. . .

Ford confirmed, "Indeed, she is."

Mistress Page, feeling a bit dramatic, said to Ford, "If you don't mind, I really must see her. I feel unwell just thinking about it." And with that, she and Robin left.

Ford was left alone, shaking his head in disbelief. "Does Page have any sense at all? Can he see what's happening right under his nose? It's as if he's blind to it all. This boy, Robin, could carry a secret message far and wide without breaking a sweat. And now, here he is, helping my wife and Mistress Page in their schemes. They think they're so clever, plotting and planning. But I see through it all. I'll expose their games, and everyone will see the truth."

Just then, the clock struck, reminding Ford it was time to act. "That's my signal," he said to himself. "I'll catch them in the act, and no one will doubt me. I'll be seen as wise, not foolish, for uncovering this."

Suddenly, Page, Shallow, Slender, and a few others arrived, greeting Ford warmly. "Good to see you, Master Ford."

Ford, trying to seem hospitable, invited them over. "I'm having a little gathering at my place. Please, join me."

. . .

Shallow declined politely, "I must say no, Master Ford."

Slender also excused himself, "I have plans with Mistress Anne. Wouldn't miss it for the world."

Shallow explained further, "We're hoping to settle a marriage proposal between Anne Page and my cousin Slender today."

Slender looked at Page, seeking his approval, "I hope you're okay with this, Father Page."

As Mistress Page and Robin prepared to leave, Mistress Page said with a playful worry, "Excuse me, sir. I won't feel better until I've seen her." With that, she and Robin headed off to see Ford's wife.

Left alone, Ford couldn't help but talk to himself, "Can Page really be so oblivious? It's like he doesn't see or think. That boy, Robin, could deliver messages with the ease of shooting arrows. He's unknowingly helping my wife and Mistress Page with their plans. Now, Mistress Page is off to see my wife with Falstaff's young helper. It's all unfolding like a poorly plotted drama."

Thinking out loud, Ford plotted, "I'll expose everyone's true colors, starting with Falstaff. My neighbors will surely support me." The chiming clock reminded him it was time to act. "The clock's chime is my cue. I'm sure Falstaff is at my house. They'll praise me for uncovering this, not mock me. Off I go."

As Ford set off, he bumped into a group including Page, Shallow, Slender, the Host, Sir Hugh Evans, Doctor Caius, and Rugby, all exchanging pleasantries.

Ford invited them home, "I've got a feast waiting, and I'll show you a monster. Doctor, you're coming. Master Page, Sir Hugh, you too."

Shallow declined, "We'll have to pass, Master Ford. We're expected elsewhere."

Ford insisted, "But you'll miss the spectacle! I have a monster at home."

The conversation shifted to Anne Page's potential marriage. Her father, Master Page, said to Slender, "You have my full support."

Doctor Caius chimed in, "And the maid loves me! Her nurse told me so."

. . .

The Host teased about another suitor, Master Fenton, "He's full of life, writes poems, dances. He's the one she'll choose."

Page firmly disagreed, "Not if I have anything to say about it. Fenton's too wild for my liking."

Ford again urged, "Come, you must all see what I've found at my house."

Curious, they agreed, "We'll come to see this monster," and they all left together, the street empty once more, echoing with the promise of an unusual discovery waiting at Ford's house.

SCENE 3

In the house of Mistress Ford, she and her friend, Mistress Page, were bustling about with a big plan in mind.

"What, John! What, Robert!" called out Mistress Ford, looking for her helpers.

"Quickly, quickly! Is the big basket ready?" Mistress Page added, eager to get moving.

"Yes, all set," Mistress Ford assured her. "And Robin, make sure you're listening!"

. . .

Just then, their servants came in, carrying a large basket. "Here, set it down here," Mistress Ford directed.

Mistress Page was all about action. "Give your men their instructions; we need to be quick about this."

Mistress Ford explained, "Like I said before, John and Robert, you need to stay close by. When I call you out suddenly, you must grab this basket without any delay and carry it on your shoulders. Then, hurry off and dump it in the muddy ditch by the river in Datchet-mead."

"Will you manage?" Mistress Page asked, wanting to be sure.

"I've told them exactly what to do. They know their task. Now, off you go and come when you're called," Mistress Ford said confidently as the servants left.

Soon, little Robin came running in.

"What's up, Robin? Any news?" greeted Mistress Ford warmly.

Robin, catching his breath, shared, "My master, Sir John, has sneaked in through the back door, Mistress Ford, and he wants to see you."

. . .

Mistress Page, curious and a bit wary, asked Robin, "Have you been loyal to us, not letting out our secret?"

"Yes, absolutely," Robin assured. "My master has no idea you're here, and he said he'd send me away forever if I told anyone about his visit. But I haven't said a word!"

Mistress Page smiled at Robin's loyalty, "You're a good boy, Robin. This secret you've kept will earn you a new outfit. Now, I'm going to hide."

Mistress Ford nodded, "Go ahead. And Robin, tell your master I'm here alone."

Once Robin left, Mistress Page made sure Mistress Ford remembered their plan, "I've got my part memorized. If I mess up, you can boo me."

Then, Mistress Page left to hide herself, and Mistress Ford prepared for their guest.

"We'll see how this trick works on him," she thought, planning to fool their visitor with a clever prank.

. . .

Just then, Falstaff entered, brimming with excitement. "Ah, my precious gem! Now I can die happy, having seen you!"

"Oh, dear Sir John!" Mistress Ford played along.

Falstaff, carried away by his feelings, confessed, "Mistress Ford, I wish your husband were out of the picture, so I could marry you!"

Mistress Ford pretended to be shocked, "Me, your wife? Oh, I wouldn't be fit for that!"

Falstaff couldn't help but praise her, "No one in France could match your beauty. Your eyes sparkle like diamonds, and your brow is perfectly shaped."

Mistress Ford humbly downplayed his compliments, "Just a simple scarf suits me best, Sir John. I'm not as grand as you say."

Falstaff insisted, "Nonsense! You'd outshine courtiers with your grace. If only fortune favored you as much as nature does."

. . .

Mistress Page, with a smile and a nod to Robin, said, "You've done well keeping our secret. Think of this as a promise for a new outfit—a thank you for your silence. Now, I'll hide."

Mistress Ford, seeing Robin off with a task, remarked, "Please tell Sir John I'm here, waiting alone." Once Robin dashed off, she turned to Mistress Page, "Remember our plan?"

"Absolutely," Mistress Page winked, "If I forget, feel free to boo me." With that, she left to hide.

Mistress Ford, alone, mused aloud, "Alright, let's see if our plan to teach a lesson works."

Falstaff soon swaggered in, overflowing with compliments. "Ah, Mistress Ford, the jewel of my heart. If this is a dream, let me never wake!"

"Oh, Sir John, you do charm," Mistress Ford replied, playing along with his game.

Falstaff's words poured out like honey. "I can't pretend, Mistress Ford. I wish your husband was out of the picture, so you could be mine."

· · ·

"To think of me as a lady? Oh, Sir John, I'd be quite the sight," Mistress Ford humored him, keeping their banter light.

"But you shine brighter than any noblewoman," Falstaff insisted, "Your grace, your beauty—no one could match it."

Mistress Ford modestly brushed aside his flattery. "A simple cloth suits me best, Sir John. Nothing more."

Falstaff, undeterred, continued, "Ah, but you're too modest. With the right chance, you'd outshine them all."

Mistress Ford deflected, "Believe me, Sir John, there's nothing of the sort in me."

"But what is it about you that has captured my heart so?" Falstaff pondered aloud. "It's beyond words, but it's there—my heart knows it."

Mistress Ford, trying to steer the conversation, expressed her worry. "But, Sir John, isn't there talk of you and Mistress Page?"

Falstaff quickly dismissed the idea. "As much as I'd like walking by a foul smell! No, it's only you, Mistress Ford."

· · ·

Their exchange was interrupted by Robin's voice, "Mistress Ford! Mistress Page is here, in quite a state, and insists on speaking with you!"

Falstaff, not wanting to be discovered, hid himself as Mistress Ford prepared to meet her friend.

Mistress Page burst in, panting and looking around wildly. "Mistress Ford, what have we done? The whole plan is on the verge of disaster!"

Mistress Ford, feigning confusion, asked, "Whatever do you mean, Mistress Page?"

"Oh, the trouble we're in! To think, with your husband such a good man, and we've given him cause to doubt," Mistress Page exclaimed.

"What cause for worry?" Mistress Ford feigned ignorance.

Mistress Page was flustered, "Can you believe it? Your husband is on his way here with the officers to search for a gentleman he thinks is hiding in your house! He believes this man is here to take advantage of his absence. You could be in big trouble."

. . .

Mistress Ford hoped that wasn't true. "Oh, I hope that's not the case."

Mistress Page urgently said, "I wish for your sake it isn't true. But your husband is definitely coming, and he's bringing a crowd to search for this man. I came ahead to warn you. If you're innocent, great. But if the man is here, you need to hide him quickly. Think about your reputation!"

"What should I do?" Mistress Ford was worried, not for herself but for her friend. "He is a dear friend, and I fear more for him than for my own embarrassment. I'd pay a lot to have him safely out of here."

Mistress Page pressed her, "There's no time for wishing. Your husband is almost here. You need to find a way to hide your friend. He can't stay in the house. Look at this basket—it might be a good hiding spot if he can fit. Or maybe your men can carry him out, hidden among the laundry."

"He won't fit in the basket. What now?" Mistress Ford panicked.

Falstaff, deciding to come out of hiding, exclaimed, "Let me see that basket! I'll try it. I'll follow your advice and hide in it."

· · ·

Mistress Page, upon seeing Falstaff trying to hide, couldn't help but mock him, "Sir John Falstaff, are you the brave knight of these letters? Trying to sneak away?"

Falstaff, desperate, pleaded, "I love you. Just help me hide. Let me get into the basket. I promise I'll—" But before he could finish, they covered him with dirty laundry.

"Quick, help cover him," Mistress Page told Robin, while Mistress Ford called for her servants, "John! Robert! Hurry!"

Robin ran off as the servants rushed in. "Take these clothes to the laundress in Datchet-meet, and fast!" Mistress Ford instructed.

Just then, Ford, Page, Doctor Caius, and Sir Hugh Evans arrived. Ford was suspicious but tried to appear calm. "If I'm wrong to suspect, then go ahead and laugh at me. I deserve it. But what's this you're carrying?"

"To the laundress," the servant innocently replied.

Ford was increasingly suspicious, not satisfied with their answers. "Why do you care where it's going? You should leave the laundry to us."

. . .

He expressed his frustration with the word "buck," hinting at his suspicion and determination to uncover the truth. As the servants left with the basket, Ford invited the others to search his house, confident they would find evidence of infidelity.

"Let's see what comes of his search," Page suggested, and they all exited to follow Ford's lead.

Alone, Mistress Page and Mistress Ford couldn't hide their delight. "Isn't this the best kind of trick?" Mistress Page beamed.

"I can't decide what's more satisfying," Mistress Ford mused, "tricking my husband or tricking Sir John." Their scheme had worked perfectly, for now.

Mistress Page couldn't help but chuckle at the memory of their recent escapade. "Oh, how flustered Sir John was when your husband inquired about the contents of the basket!"

Mistress Ford joined in the laughter, albeit with a hint of concern. "I worry the poor man might need a real wash after all that commotion. Perhaps being tossed into the water might actually do him some good."

. . .

"Him, a dishonest trickster! I wish all men who act like him could find themselves in the same pickle," Mistress Page exclaimed with a mix of amusement and disdain.

Mistress Ford pondered their next move. "I suspect my husband is becoming suspicious of Falstaff's visits. I've never seen him this upset by jealousy before."

Mistress Page, always one step ahead, plotted further mischief. "Let's test my husband's suspicions further and have some more fun with Falstaff. He hardly learns from his mistakes, does he?"

"Perhaps we should involve Mistress Quickly in our next scheme, suggest to Falstaff that his dunking was all for the best, and then lure him into another trap," Mistress Ford suggested with a mischievous glint in her eye.

"Perfect," agreed Mistress Page. "Let's have Falstaff summoned tomorrow at eight for his 'apology.'"

Just then, Ford, Page, Doctor Caius, and Sir Hugh Evans re-entered, their search fruitless. Ford, somewhat defeated, mused aloud that perhaps he had been led on a wild goose chase.

. . .

Mistress Ford and Mistress Page exchanged knowing looks, barely containing their mirth.

"Do you find me a fool, Master Ford? Do you treat me kindly?" Mistress Ford asked, her voice dripping with irony.

Ford, oblivious to the underlying tone, assured her of his good intentions. "Of course, I do."

"May heaven help you to improve," Mistress Ford retorted, her patience thinning.

Mistress Page couldn't resist adding her two cents, suggesting Ford was being unfair to himself with his unwarranted jealousy.

Ford resignedly accepted the criticism. "I suppose I must endure it."

Sir Hugh Evans, perhaps feeling a moment of pious reflection amid the chaos, expressed a hope for divine forgiveness if there were any hidden secrets within the house, unknowingly brushing against the truth of the recent antics.

· · ·

Mistress Page and Mistress Ford, sharing a laugh at the chaos, couldn't believe how flustered Falstaff was when Ford inquired about the basket's contents. "Imagine his panic!" Mistress Page said, almost gleefully.

Mistress Ford, half-joking, half-serious, added, "He might need a wash after all this. A dip in the river could be just what he needs."

They both agreed that anyone as deceitful as Falstaff deserved a bit of trouble. "I wish all tricksters found themselves in such a bind," Mistress Page declared.

Mistress Ford then voiced a concern, "I think my husband suspects something about Falstaff. He's never been so intensely jealous."

"Not to worry," Mistress Page plotted, "we'll come up with more schemes to trick Falstaff. He won't know what hit him."

They even considered sending Mistress Quickly to Falstaff with a made-up story to set him up for another round of their game.

Ford, Page, Doctor Caius, and Sir Hugh Evans came back, unable to find Falstaff. Ford seemed to regret his suspicions and actions, acknowledging his mistake.

. . .

Page and the others chided Ford for his wild imagination and praised Mistress Ford's honesty. They all decided to move past the incident, with Ford inviting everyone for a meal as a peace offering.

The group made plans for the next day, hinting at more adventures and possibly more pranks on their unsuspecting host, all in good humor and fellowship, leaving the day's mischief behind.

SCENE 4

In a cozy room at Page's house, Fenton and Anne Page had a serious conversation. Fenton sadly said, "I see I can't win your father's love, so don't try to convince him about me anymore, dear Nan."

Anne, worried, asked, "Oh, what should we do then?"

Fenton replied, "You just need to be yourself. Your dad thinks I'm too fancy for you and that I'm only after his money because I've spent too much of mine. He also doesn't like my past wild friends. He thinks I can't really love you, just see you as something to own."

Anne thought for a moment and said, "Maybe he's right."

. . .

"No, I hope to prove him wrong," Fenton passionately responded. "At first, I was interested in your family's wealth, but as I got to know you, Anne, I realized you're worth more than all the gold in the world. It's you I care about, not the money."

Anne, touched by his words, suggested, "Master Fenton, please keep trying to win my father's love. If you can't, well, we'll think of something else."

Just then, Shallow, Slender, and Mistress Quickly walked in. Shallow, wanting to interrupt, said to Mistress Quickly, "Break up their chat. Let my cousin speak for himself."

Slender, trying to be brave, declared, "I'll take my chance, though it's a bit scary."

"Don't be scared," Shallow encouraged him.

Slender admitted, "I'm not scared of her saying no. I'm just naturally scared."

Mistress Quickly, trying to help things along, said to Anne, "Master Slender wants to talk to you."

· · ·

Anne went over to him, thinking to herself, "This is who my father wants me to marry. It's amazing what looks good when there's money involved."

Mistress Quickly, not wanting to leave anyone out, then turned to Fenton, "And how are you, Master Fenton? Can we chat for a moment?"

Meanwhile, Shallow was encouraging Slender, "She's coming to talk to you. Oh, if only your father could see you now!"

Slender, a bit nervous, said, "I did have a father, Mistress Anne. My uncle here can tell you some funny stories about him. Please, uncle, tell her about the time my father took two geese from a pen."

Shallow, trying to steer the conversation back, told Anne, "My cousin really likes you."

Slender chimed in, "Yes, I do. As much as I like any woman in Gloucestershire."

Shallow added, "He'll take good care of you, like a true gentleman."

. . .

Slender promised, "Yes, I will. No matter what, I'll make sure you're well looked after."

Shallow even promised a dowry, "He will give you a hundred and fifty pounds as a jointure."

Anne, wanting Slender to speak for himself, said, "Good Master Shallow, let him woo for himself."

Shallow took the hint, "Well, I appreciate that. Good luck, cousin," and left them to talk.

Now alone, Anne asked, "Now, Master Slender, what did you want to say?"

Slender, a bit confused, said, "What is my will? That's funny! I haven't made a will yet, thank goodness. I'm not planning on leaving just yet!"

Anne, trying to understand, asked, "What do you want from me, Master Slender?"

Slender honestly replied, "Honestly, I don't have much to say. Your dad and my uncle have been discussing this. If it turns out I'm lucky, great; if not, well, someone else will be happy. They know more about this than I do. You should talk to your dad; oh, look, here he comes."

As they were speaking, Page and Mistress Page walked in. Page saw Slender and said, "Love him, daughter Anne. And Fenton, what are you doing here again? I've already told you my daughter is promised to another."

Fenton tried to calm him, "Please, Master Page, don't be upset."

Mistress Page also warned Fenton, "Please, don't come around my daughter."

Page was firm, "She's not for you, Fenton."

Fenton tried to argue, "But, sir, if you'd just listen—"

"No," Page interrupted, "Come, Master Shallow, and you, son Slender, inside. Fenton, you know my stance. You're wrong to keep bothering us." Then Page, Shallow, and Slender left.

Mistress Quickly suggested to Fenton, "Talk to Mistress Page."

. . .

Fenton, not giving up, told her, "I truly love your daughter in a good and honest way, and I must show my love openly, despite any objections. I hope for your support."

Anne, not wanting to marry Slender, pleaded with her mom, "Please, don't make me marry that fool."

Mistress Page reassured her, "I won't. I'm looking for a better husband for you."

Mistress Quickly then hinted, "That would be my master, the doctor."

Mistress Quickly, watching the scene unfold, spoke up, "I played a part in this, you know. I told them, 'Why waste your daughter on a fool or a doctor when there's Master Fenton?' I helped make this happen."

Fenton, grateful for her support, gave her a ring, "Thank you, Mistress Quickly. Please, could you give this ring to sweet Nan for me? It's a small token for your trouble."

Mistress Quickly, beaming with pride, responded, "May good luck follow you, Master Fenton! You're a true gentleman."

. . .

After Fenton left, Mistress Quickly mused to herself, "He's got such a kind heart. Anyone would be lucky to have him. I hope it works out for him, Master Slender, or even my own master. I've promised to help all three, and I'll keep my word. But my heart's really set on helping Master Fenton."

Then, as if remembering something urgent, she exclaimed, "Oh, I've got another message to deliver to Sir John Falstaff from my mistresses. I can't believe I almost forgot. I better hurry!"

With that, Mistress Quickly rushed off to fulfill her next errand, her mind a whirlwind of matchmaking plans and promises.

SCENE 5

In a cozy room within the Garter Inn, Sir John Falstaff, a portly and jovial man, was having a lively chat with his friend Bardolph, a man with a bright red nose.

"Falstaff: Bardolph, could you fetch me a big cup of sweet wine and pop a piece of toast in it?" Falstaff asked, craving a warm drink.

"Certainly, sir," Bardolph replied before leaving to fulfill the request.

Left alone, Falstaff couldn't help but muse over his recent misadventures. "Can you believe it? I ended up being carted off in a basket like a bunch of unwanted scraps and tossed into the Thames River! If they try such a stunt again, I swear I'll feed my brains to a dog as a holiday treat. They dumped me into the water as easily as if I were nothing more than unwanted puppies. And given how big I am, I sink rather quickly. I was lucky the river was shallow where I landed, or I would have been a goner. Imagine how bloated I would have looked if I'd been submerged for too long!"

Just then, Bardolph returned with the sweet wine, interrupting Falstaff's grumbling.

"Bardolph: Sir, Mistress Quickly wishes to speak with you," he announced, bringing in the drink.

"Ah, let's add some of this wine to warm me up. It feels as though I've swallowed snowballs instead! Invite her in," Falstaff said, trying to shake off the chill.

Bardolph called out, "Come in, ma'am!"

Mistress Quickly, a lively woman, entered the room. "Good morning, sir! I hope I'm not intruding," she greeted Falstaff with a polite nod.

"Falstaff: Bardolph, take these cups away and make me a large pot of sweet wine, but keep it simple this time," Falstaff ordered, then turned to Mistress Quickly. "So, what brings you here today?"

Bardolph, ever the helper, asked, "With eggs, sir?"

"Just the wine," Falstaff insisted, eager for a drink that wasn't too fancy.

As Bardolph left to prepare the drink, Mistress Quickly got straight to the point. "Sir, I've come on behalf of Mistress Ford to see you," she said, bringing a message from another friend.

Falstaff, still feeling the effects of his chilly dip in the river, replied with a touch of humor, "Mistress Ford? After my recent dunking in the ford, I feel I've had quite enough of fords and rivers for a while!"

Mistress Quickly, looking quite serious, said to Falstaff, "Oh dear, it wasn't her fault at all. She's quite upset about the mix-up; it would make you feel sorry to see her so sad. Her husband went out early this morning, and she really wants to see you again between eight and nine. She said she'd make it up to you, I promise."

Falstaff, intrigued by the message, decided, "Alright, I'll go see her. Tell her to think about what being a person is all about, to remember we all make mistakes, and then she can see if I'm worth her time."

"I'll make sure to tell her exactly that," Mistress Quickly assured him.

"And you said between nine and ten, right?" Falstaff wanted to be certain of the time.

"No, sir, between eight and nine," she corrected him.

"Okay, then. I won't miss it," Falstaff confirmed, ready for the appointment.

"Wishing you peace, sir," Mistress Quickly said as she left.

Alone again, Falstaff wondered why he hadn't heard from Master Brook, who was very interested in Falstaff's dealings and had plenty of money to offer for information. Just then, Ford, who was secretly Master Brook, arrived.

"Hello, sir!" Ford greeted him cheerfully.

. . .

Falstaff, recognizing him, jumped straight to the point, "Ah, Master Brook, you're here to find out what happened with Mistress Ford?"

"Yes, Sir John, I'm eager to hear about it," Ford replied, curious about the details.

Falstaff, with a hint of disappointment, admitted, "Well, I won't lie to you. I did go to her house when she asked me to."

"And how did it go, sir?" Ford asked, hoping for good news.

"Unfortunately, not well at all, Master Brook," Falstaff sighed, sharing his unfortunate experience.

Falstaff continued to share his wild tale with Ford, who listened with growing amazement.

"Falstaff: No, Master Brook, the problem wasn't her changing her mind. It was her husband, Mr. Ford, who's always suspicious, bursting in just as we were getting acquainted. He was followed by a crowd, all stirred up by his jealous nature, and they began searching the house for me!"

· · ·

"Ford: They did? While you were still there?" Ford asked, his curiosity piqued.

"Yes, right while I was there. But then, Mrs. Page came in and warned us. Mrs. Ford's quick thinking and her distraction helped hide me in a laundry basket full of dirty clothes," Falstaff explained, chuckling at the memory.

"A laundry basket!" Ford exclaimed, hardly believing what he was hearing.

"Exactly, a laundry basket! I was squished in with all the stinky shirts, socks, and napkins. It was the worst smell I've ever experienced," Falstaff recounted, making a face.

"And how long were you in there?" Ford pressed, eager for more details.

Falstaff leaned in, ready to share the most unbelievable part. "You won't believe what I went through to help you. They carried me out, pretending I was just a load of laundry, right past Mr. Ford. He even asked what was in the basket but never thought to check. My heart was racing, fearing he'd find me. But luck was on my side, and they took me all the way to Datchet-lane."

. . .

Ford was astounded. "All that just to avoid being caught?"

"Yes, but it gets worse. Imagine, a man like me, trapped in that basket, scared out of my wits, then drenched in the Thames to cool off. It was a narrow escape from being cooked alive!" Falstaff concluded, shaking his head at the sheer absurdity of his adventure.

Ford couldn't help but marvel at Falstaff's escapade, a mix of disbelief and awe in his eyes.

Ford listened with a mixture of regret and determination as Falstaff vowed not to give up on his pursuit, despite the risks and discomforts he had already faced.

"Falstaff: Trust me, Master Brook, I'd rather jump into a volcano than give up now. Her husband went out this morning, and she's asked me to meet her again soon," Falstaff declared with resolve.

"Ford: But it's already past the time she mentioned," Ford pointed out, worried about the ticking clock.

"Is it? Then I must hurry to see her. After our meeting, come see me when you can, and I'll tell you all about it. Hopefully, I'll have good news for you," Falstaff said confidently, then added, "Farewell. You'll get what you wish for, Master Brook."

With that, Falstaff left, leaving Ford alone with his thoughts.

Ford pondered the situation, bewildered and conflicted. "Is this real? Am I dreaming? Wake up, Ford! Your plan is unfolding, but at what cost? To think, all of this trouble over a mischievous plan!"

Resolved yet troubled, Ford decided to take action. "I must face this challenge head-on. I will catch Falstaff myself. He won't be able to hide from me, no matter where he tries to sneak off to. I refuse to be made a fool of. Even if I must face my fears, I won't be brought down by them."

With determination fueling his steps, Ford set off to confront the situation, ready to face whatever came next, even if it meant embracing his own anger and frustration.

ACT IV

SCENE 1

On a bright morning, Mistress Page, Mistress Quickly, and young William strolled down the bustling street. They were deep in conversation.

"Has he made it to Master Ford's house yet, do you think?" Mistress Page asked, a hint of curiosity in her voice.

"Oh, certainly! If not now, then very soon," Mistress Quickly replied with confidence. "But let me tell you, he's quite upset about being tossed into the water. Mistress Ford is eagerly waiting for you to drop by."

"I'll visit her shortly; I just need to take William here to his lessons first. Oh, look! Here comes his teacher, Sir Hugh. It looks like it's a day off from lessons," Mistress Page noted, spotting Sir Hugh approaching.

As Sir Hugh joined them, Mistress Page couldn't help but ask, "Sir Hugh, no lessons today?"

"Indeed, no lessons. Master Slender has given the boys a day off to play," Sir Hugh explained with a gentle smile.

Mistress Quickly exclaimed, "What a kind heart he has!"

Turning her attention back to Sir Hugh, Mistress Page expressed her concern. "Sir Hugh, my husband and I worry that William isn't really learning much. Could you test his knowledge a bit, perhaps?"

"Of course," Sir Hugh agreed, turning to William. "Come here, young man. Don't be shy. Let's see what you've learned."

William stepped forward, a bit nervous but ready.

"William, can you tell me how many forms nouns can have?" Sir Hugh asked, starting with the basics.

· · ·

"Two," William answered quickly, gaining a bit of confidence.

Mistress Quickly, always ready with a comment, added, "I would've thought there was one more, given how often I hear 'Od's nouns.'"

Sir Hugh, trying to maintain focus, shifted the topic. "Let's keep on track. William, what does 'fair' mean?"

"Pulcher," William replied, showcasing his learning.

Laughing, Mistress Quickly chimed in, "Well, I dare say there are things much fairer than polecats!"

Their laughter filled the street as they enjoyed this brief moment of learning and jest before continuing on their way.

Sir Hugh, trying to continue the lesson, chuckled lightly at the jests but wished to bring focus back to William's education. "You do love a good laugh, but let's concentrate on the lesson. Now, William, what does 'lapis' mean?"

William thought for a moment before answering, "A stone."

. . .

"And can you tell me, what is 'a stone' in another way?" Sir Hugh probed further, guiding William's learning.

"A pebble?" William guessed, looking up at Sir Hugh for confirmation.

Sir Hugh shook his head gently, "No, no. 'Lapis' itself means stone. Always remember that, William."

"Lapis," William repeated, nodding his understanding.

"Very good, William. Now, who is it that lends articles?" Sir Hugh moved on to a more complex concept.

William straightened up, ready with his answer, "Articles are borrowed from the pronoun and can be declined like this: Singulariter, nominativo, hic, haec, hoc."

Sir Hugh corrected him with a rhyme to make it easier, "Nominativo, hig, hag, hog; remember that, William. And what about the genitive case?"

"Genitivo, hujus," William responded, his confidence growing.

· · ·

"And your accusative case?" Sir Hugh asked, encouraging William to think.

"Accusativo, hinc," William said, but Sir Hugh corrected him softly, "Remember, it's accusative, hung, hang, hog."

Mistress Quickly couldn't resist adding her humor, "Hang-hog must be Latin for bacon, I bet."

Sir Hugh, slightly exasperated but still patient, asked, "And the vocative case, William?"

"O,--vocativo, O," William answered correctly this time.

"Remember, William, vocative often doesn't change. It's a special case," Sir Hugh explained, trying to simplify the concept.

Mistress Quickly joked again, "And that's the root of all goodness."

"Please, let's try to focus," Sir Hugh sighed, then asked William another question, "What about the genitive case plural?"

. . .

William, thinking hard, finally said, "Genitive,--horum, harum, horum."

Mistress Quickly, always ready with a sharp comment, suddenly blurted out, "Never mention that Jenny! If she's not nice, don't even say her name, child."

Sir Hugh, a bit shocked, scolded her gently, "For shame, please don't use such words."

But Mistress Quickly was not done. "It's wrong to fill the child's head with such nonsense," she protested. "Teaching him all these complicated words will only confuse him more!"

Sir Hugh, bewildered by her outburst, couldn't help but question her understanding. "Do you not see the importance of learning the proper terms for things? Your approach is more confusing than helpful."

Mistress Page, trying to ease the tension, suggested they calm down.

Ignoring the squabble, Sir Hugh turned back to William, eager to continue the lesson. "Can you show me how you decline pronouns, William?"

. . .

William, perhaps a little distracted by the adults' argument, admitted, "Honestly, I've forgotten."

"It's simple," Sir Hugh reminded him kindly. "Qui, quae, quod. Remember, forgetting these basics will only make learning harder. Now, off you go and enjoy your playtime."

Mistress Page watched the exchange, impressed. "He knows more than I realized."

Sir Hugh, pleased with William's effort despite the forgetfulness, bid farewell. "He has a sharp mind. Goodbye, Mistress Page."

"Goodbye, Sir Hugh," she replied, as Sir Hugh departed.

Turning to William, she decided it was time to head back. "Let's go home, boy. We've been here long enough."

And with that, they left, the morning's lesson concluding with laughter, a bit of scolding, and the promise of more learning to come.

SCENE 2

In a cozy room within Ford's house, Sir John Falstaff and Mistress Ford were having a heartfelt conversation.

Falstaff, with a twinkle in his eye, spoke gently, "Mistress Ford, it seems your sadness is very deep. I see you really care, and I promise to match your feelings exactly. It's not just about being friends, but about everything that comes with it. Is your husband not around?"

Mistress Ford replied with a light laugh, "He's out bird watching, dear Sir John."

Just then, they heard Mistress Page's voice from outside, calling, "Hello, Mistress Ford! Are you there?"

. . .

Mistress Ford quickly whispered to Falstaff, "Please, hide in the next room, Sir John." And with that, Falstaff stepped away.

Mistress Page entered the room, looking around with curiosity. "Hello, dear! Is anyone else here with you?"

"Just my family," Mistress Ford answered, trying to seem casual.

"Really?" asked Mistress Page, not quite convinced.

"Yes, really," Mistress Ford insisted, hinting for her friend to speak up a bit more.

Mistress Page, now a bit more relaxed, shared her relief. "I'm so glad there's no one else here."

"Why do you ask?" inquired Mistress Ford, puzzled.

Mistress Page leaned in closer and explained, "Well, your husband is caught up in one of his moods again. He's been making a fuss with my husband, complaining about all sorts of things, blaming all of marriage, and even acting a bit silly, saying 'Look out, look out!' in such a frenzy. It's unlike anything I've seen before; it makes his usual grumbles seem quite mild. I'm just glad that Sir John isn't here to see this."

Mistress Ford, looking worried, asked, "Why, is he talking about Sir John?"

Mistress Page nodded, "Yes, he keeps talking about him. He even said he was once carried out in a basket when they were looking for him! He's convinced Sir John is here now and has even pulled his friends from their fun to search again. But I'm glad Sir John isn't here; my husband will only end up embarrassing himself."

"How close is he?" Mistress Ford's voice trembled a little.

"Just down the street; he'll be here any minute," Mistress Page informed.

Mistress Ford panicked, "Oh no, Sir John is actually here!"

"Well, then it's better to face a little embarrassment than something worse," Mistress Page tried to reassure her. "What are we going to do with him?"

· · ·

As they pondered their next move, Falstaff reappeared, "I won't hide in that basket again. Can't I just leave before he gets here?"

Mistress Page shook her head, "That's not possible. Three of Master Ford's brothers are guarding the door with their pistols, making sure no one leaves. But why did you come back?"

Falstaff, desperate, suggested, "What if I hide in the chimney?"

"That won't work; they use it for shooting practice," Mistress Ford quickly said. "Try the kiln-hole."

"But won't he look there?" Falstaff was getting more anxious.

Mistress Ford sighed, "He knows every possible hiding spot in this house and checks them all. There's no way to hide you here."

"I'll have to leave, then," Falstaff decided, seeing no other choice. Their conversation was filled with hurried whispers and frantic planning, trying to outwit an unexpected visit that threatened to unravel their secret.

. . .

Mistress Page, with a worried look, warned, "If you step outside as you are, Sir John, it's all over for you. Unless you disguise yourself..."

"How can we disguise him?" Mistress Ford pondered aloud.

"Oh dear, I'm not sure!" Mistress Page exclaimed. "If only we had a dress large enough for him, or he could wear a hat, a scarf, and a kerchief to cover his face and escape."

Falstaff, looking desperate, pleaded, "Please, think of something! I'd do anything to avoid trouble."

Mistress Ford then had an idea, "My maid's aunt, the large lady from Brentford, has a gown that could fit you."

"Yes, that could work! She's about your size, and she even has a thick hat and scarf," Mistress Page added excitedly. "Hurry upstairs, Sir John!"

"Off you go, dear Sir John. Mistress Page and I will find something to cover your head," Mistress Ford encouraged.

"Quickly, quickly! We'll help you dress in no time. Put on the gown for now," Mistress Page urged as Falstaff hurried off.

. . .

Mistress Ford then shared a hopeful thought, "I wish my husband could see him dressed like this. He can't stand the old woman of Brentford; he thinks she's a witch and has even banned her from our house."

Mistress Page chuckled, "Let's hope he runs into my husband's stick then. It would be quite the sight!"

"But is my husband really coming?" Mistress Ford asked, growing anxious.

"Yes, sadly, he is. And he's still talking about that basket trick," Mistress Page replied.

"Well, let's see if we can trick him again. I'll have my men ready with the basket to surprise him at the door, just like last time," Mistress Ford schemed, as they both hurried off to prepare their plan and help their friend, Sir John, avoid a sticky situation.

In the midst of their hurried plans, Mistress Page said with a hint of excitement, "Let's go dress him up like the Brentford witch, quickly!"

. . .

Mistress Ford, already thinking ahead, replied, "I'll go tell my servants what to do with that big basket. You start dressing him up; I'll bring the clothes for Sir John in a minute." And off she went.

Mistress Page, alone for a moment, mumbled to herself with a grin, "That sneaky man, we'll teach him a lesson. We're going to prove that wives can have their fun and still be true. It's an old saying, but it still rings true: Sometimes you have to stir the pot to keep things interesting."

Then, Mistress Ford came back, her arms full of linen, instructing her servants with urgency, "Take the basket again on your shoulders. My husband will be here any moment. If he tells you to put it down, just do it quickly and get out of there." She shooed them off just as her husband and his friends were about to arrive.

One servant whispered to the other as they lifted the basket, "I hope it's not another trick with the knight hidden inside."

"I'd rather carry bricks than be part of another one of their schemes," his companion grumbled.

Just then, Ford burst onto the scene with his friends, determined to uncover the truth. "If your sneaky tricks are real, Master Page, how will you make me look a fool again? Drop that basket, you rogues! Call out my wife. I want to see what's really going on," Ford demanded, his voice filled with suspicion and frustration.

Page, witnessing the chaos, couldn't help but comment, "This is getting out of hand, Ford. You can't keep doubting everything and everyone."

Sir Hugh Evans shook his head in disbelief, "This is madness, pure madness!"

They all watched, holding their breaths, as the scene unfolded, wondering if this time Ford's suspicions would finally be proven right or if it was just another wild goose chase fueled by jealousy and confusion.

As the tension rose, Master Shallow couldn't help but express his concern, "Truly, Master Ford, this doesn't look good."

Ford, caught up in his suspicions, barely acknowledged Shallow's words. Just then, Mistress Ford re-entered the scene, and Ford, with a hint of sarcasm, called out to her, "Oh, come here, Mistress Ford, the picture of honesty, the epitome of a virtuous wife, who has the misfortune of being married to a fool consumed by jealousy! I'm wrong to doubt you, am I not?"

· · ·

Mistress Ford, standing her ground, replied earnestly, "I swear, you are mistaken if you think I've been unfaithful."

Ford, not convinced, retorted sharply, "Well spoken, shameless one! Keep up your act. Now, come out, you scoundrel!" as he began to rummage through the clothes in the basket.

Page, watching the spectacle, exclaimed, "This is outrageous!"

Mistress Ford, embarrassed and frustrated, pleaded, "Aren't you embarrassed? Leave those clothes alone."

But Ford was relentless, "I'll find him soon enough."

Sir Hugh Evans tried to intervene, "This is madness! Why are you dragging out your wife's clothes? Let's leave this alone."

Ford, however, was determined, "Empty the basket, I demand it!"

Mistress Ford, confused and upset, questioned, "Why are you doing this?"

. . .

Ford explained his reasoning, fueled by his previous suspicions, "Master Page, believe me, there was a man sneaked out in this basket from my house just yesterday. Why couldn't he be there again? I'm certain he's here; my suspicions are justified. Empty out all the linen."

"If you find a man there, he's as good as a goner," Mistress Ford declared defiantly.

But Page, having checked the basket, confirmed, "There's no man here."

Shallow, feeling sorry for Ford's plight, added, "This is truly not right, Master Ford. You're doing yourself wrong here."

Sir Hugh Evans offered some advice amidst the chaos, "Master Ford, you need to pray and not let your heart be led by these unfounded fears. This is nothing but jealousy."

Ford, still not convinced, insisted, "He's not here, but I must keep looking."

Page, trying to calm him, pointed out, "He's not here, or anywhere. You're imagining things."

· · ·

Ford, desperate for proof, pleaded, "Help me search my house one more time. If we find nothing, I'll accept any ridicule. Just help me search again."

Just then, Mistress Ford called out, hoping to divert her husband's suspicion, "Mistress Page, please bring down the old woman; my husband wants to check the chamber."

Ford, puzzled, asked, "Old woman? What old woman?"

Mistress Ford quickly replied, "It's just my maid's aunt from Brentford."

Ford, growing more agitated, exclaimed, "A witch, that's what she is! I've told her to stay away from our home. She's up to no good, claiming to tell fortunes. I want her out!"

Mistress Ford, trying to prevent any harm, pleaded, "Please, be kind! Don't hurt the old woman."

Then, re-entered Falstaff, disguised in women's clothes, with Mistress Page calling to him, "Come here, Mother Prat, let's go."

· · ·

Ford, not recognizing Falstaff and thinking him the witch, angrily chased him out, shouting insults and threatening to "conjure" him away.

After Falstaff hurriedly exited, Mistress Page turned to Ford, "Aren't you ashamed? You might have hurt that poor woman."

Ford, still wrapped up in his suspicion and confusion, declared his intention to rid his house of what he believed to be a witch, referring to Falstaff disguised in women's clothes. "She's nothing but a witch!" he exclaimed.

Sir Hugh Evans, puzzled by the sight before him, remarked, "I swear, this woman must truly be a witch. Did anyone else see the beard under her scarf?"

Ford, eager to prove his point, urged his friends, "Come, follow me. Let's see where this goes. If I'm wrong, then never listen to me again."

Page, always the peacemaker, suggested, "Let's indulge him a little longer and see what happens."

After the men left in pursuit of Falstaff, Mistress Page turned to Mistress Ford, shaking her head, "He really gave him a thrashing, didn't he?"

. . .

Mistress Ford replied with a mixture of amusement and disbelief, "It was hardly a fair fight, the way he went after him."

Mistress Page, with a twinkle in her eye, suggested, "We should celebrate that cudgel; it's done us a great service today."

Then, contemplating their next move, Mistress Ford pondered, "Do you think we should go any further with our revenge, or have we scared him enough?"

Mistress Page confidently replied, "I think he's learned his lesson. He wouldn't dare trouble us again."

The two women then contemplated whether to share their adventure with their husbands. "Should we tell our husbands how we tricked him?" Mistress Ford asked.

"Absolutely," Mistress Page agreed. "It might just clear up any misunderstandings they have about the whole affair."

Mistress Ford smiled, imagining the outcome. "They'll probably want to shame him publicly for this."

. . .

Mistress Page nodded, "Then let's not waste any time. We should act while the story is still fresh."

With that, the two women exited, planning their next steps and ready to share their victorious tale, having outwitted Falstaff in a most amusing and memorable fashion.

SCENE 3

I n a cozy room inside the Garter Inn, the owner of the inn
was talking with a man named Bardolph.

"Sir, some German visitors want to borrow three of your
horses," Bardolph explained. "The duke himself is coming to
town tomorrow, and they want to go greet him."

The innkeeper raised an eyebrow, puzzled. "What duke is this,
sneaking around so quietly? I haven't heard anything about
him being here. Do these gentlemen speak English?"

"Yes, sir; they do. Shall I bring them to you?" Bardolph asked.

. . .

The innkeeper nodded. "Sure, let them have my horses. But they will have to pay a good price. They've been staying in my inn for a week now, making me send away my other guests. They should be ready to pay for such favors. Let's go and talk to them."

With that, they both left the room to meet the guests.

SCENE 4

I n Ford's house, friends and family gathered, all buzzing with plans and news. Sir Hugh Evans complimented a lady, saying she was one of the wisest women he'd ever met.

Page turned to the ladies, curious. "Did he really send both letters at the same time?"

"Yep, all within fifteen minutes," Mistress Page confirmed.

Ford, feeling a bit guilty, turned to his wife. "I'm sorry, dear. From now on, you do what you think is best. I trust you more than anything. I know now you're as true and steadfast as anyone could be."

· · ·

Page nodded in agreement but advised, "Let's not go overboard, okay? But yes, let's continue with our plan. Let's trick him one more time, catch him in the act, and show everyone what he's really like."

Ford liked the idea. "That's the best plan yet."

Page was a bit skeptical, "You think he'll actually come to the park at midnight? I doubt it."

Sir Hugh Evans added, "After all the trouble he's been through, I'd be surprised if he dared show his face."

Mistress Ford was already thinking ahead. "Let's just figure out what to do when he shows up, and we'll make sure he gets here."

Mistress Page shared a spooky story to set their trap. "There's a legend about Herne the Hunter, who haunts the Windsor forest, especially around a certain oak tree. They say he causes all sorts of trouble there. Everyone's heard the tales, and many believe them to be true."

They all nodded, getting more excited about their plan, using the old stories to their advantage.

· · ·

Page was intrigued, "So, people are actually scared to walk by that tree at night?"

Mistress Ford nodded, "Exactly! And we're going to have Falstaff meet us there."

Page was convinced, "He'll definitely show up. But once we get him there, what's the next step? What's the plan?"

Mistress Page shared their creative scheme, "We've got it all figured out. My daughter Nan, my little son, and a few of their friends will dress up as little elves and fairies, wearing green and white. They'll have candles on their heads and rattles in their hands. When Falstaff meets us, these 'fairies' will suddenly jump out, singing and making a grand entrance. We'll pretend to be scared and run away."

Mistress Ford continued, "Then, the kids will surround him, pretending to be fairies punishing him for trespassing on their magical time. They'll pretend to pinch him and scare him with their candles until he promises to tell the truth."

Mistress Page added, "Once he admits what he's been up to, we'll all reveal ourselves, take off our disguises, and have a good laugh as we escort him back to town."

. . .

Ford was practical, "We need to make sure the kids know exactly what to do."

Sir Hugh Evans was eager to help, "I'll teach the kids their parts. And I'll join in too, helping to tease the knight with my candle."

Page, looking around at the eager faces, chuckled. "There are plenty who'd be scared to walk by Herne's oak at night. But what's the plan?"

Mistress Ford, with a glint in her eye, replied, "Our plan is simple. We'll have Falstaff meet us by that very oak."

Page nodded, getting into the spirit. "He'll show up, no doubt. But once we've got him there, in all his confusion, what then? What's the grand plan?"

Mistress Page, ever the planner, laid it out. "Here's what we'll do: my daughter Nan, my little boy, and a few of their friends will dress up as fairies and sprites, all in green and white. They'll wear crowns of candles and carry rattles. As soon as Falstaff meets us, these 'fairies' will rush out, singing and dancing. We'll act shocked and run away, leaving them to circle Falstaff, teasing him and demanding to know why he dares to join their fairy revels."

· · ·

Mistress Ford added, "And they won't stop until he tells the truth. They'll pinch him and light him up with their candles!"

Mistress Page concluded with a smile, "Once he confesses, we'll reveal ourselves, unmask the ghostly guise, and laugh him all the way back to Windsor."

Ford was practical. "The kids need to practice to pull this off."

Sir Hugh Evans, ever enthusiastic, volunteered, "I'll teach them their parts. I'll even play along, scaring Falstaff with my own lantern."

Ford was already on his feet. "Brilliant! I'll go buy masks for everyone."

Mistress Page, thinking ahead, declared, "And my Nan will be the fairy queen, dressed in white silk."

Page, with a secretive grin, whispered, "While you're all busy, Master Slender will whisk Nan away and marry her. But let's get Falstaff on board first."

Ford, determined, added, "I'll talk to him as Brook again. He'll spill his plans, sure as day."

. . .

Mistress Page urged, "Don't worry about him showing up. Let's focus on getting our fairy costumes ready."

Sir Hugh Evans summed up their mood, "Let's get to it. It'll be great fun and quite the clever trick."

As they dispersed to set their plan in motion, Mistress Page sent Mistress Ford to hurry and invite Falstaff, while she herself went to ensure Doctor Caius would marry her daughter, dismissing Slender as a foolish choice. The plot thickened, everyone excited for the impending comedic chaos.

SCENE 5

I n a cozy room at the Garter Inn, the Innkeeper greeted a visitor named Simple.

"What can I do for you?" the Innkeeper asked. "Speak up, let's make it quick!"

Simple, a bit hesitant, replied, "Well, sir, I'm here to see Sir John Falstaff. Master Slender sent me."

The Innkeeper nodded, "You'll find him upstairs. His room is easy to find; it's the one with the Prodigal Son painting. Go ahead and knock."

. . .

Simple looked a bit worried, "Actually, there's a lady who went up to see him just now. I think I'll wait until she comes back down. I need to talk to her."

The Innkeeper, surprised, exclaimed, "A lady? We should check on Sir John then!" He called out loudly, hoping Sir John would hear, "Sir John, are you up there? It's your host calling!"

From upstairs, Falstaff's voice came down, "What's happening, my good host?"

The Innkeeper explained to Sir John about the visitor waiting for the lady to come down. "We must maintain our honor here; please send her down," he added.

Falstaff soon joined them downstairs and said, "Ah, the lady you're talking about just left. She was here, but she's gone now."

Simple, curious, asked, "Was it the wise woman from Brentford?"

"Yes, that's right," Falstaff answered. "What do you want with her?"

. . .

Simple explained, "My master, Master Slender, saw her walking through the streets and wanted to know if a man named Nym, who took his chain, still had it or not."

Falstaff shared with Simple, "I talked to the old lady about the chain."

"What did she say?" Simple eagerly asked.

"She said the same man who tricked Master Slender and took his chain was the one who really did it," Falstaff explained.

Simple sighed, "I wish I could've spoken to her myself. There were other things Master Slender wanted me to ask."

"Like what? Tell us," Falstaff encouraged.

The Innkeeper joined in, "Yes, let's hear it, quickly!"

Simple hesitated, "I'm not supposed to hide them, sir."

"Hide them or you'll be in trouble," the Innkeeper half-joked.

· · ·

"Well, it was about Miss Anne Page. My master wanted to know if he had a chance with her," Simple finally said.

Falstaff nodded, "Yes, he does have a chance."

"Really, sir?" Simple was surprised.

"Yes, tell your master that the lady said so," Falstaff confirmed.

Simple was relieved, "Thank you, sir! This will make my master very happy."

As Simple left to share the news with his master, the Innkeeper complimented Falstaff, "You're quite the scholar, Sir John. Was there really a wise woman?"

"Yes, there was," Falstaff grinned. "She taught me more than I've ever learned, and it didn't cost me anything. In fact, I got paid for learning!"

Just then, Bardolph rushed in, upset, "Oh no, sir! It's a disaster!"

. . .

"What about my horses?" the Innkeeper asked, concerned about his property.

Falstaff shared with Simple, "I talked to the wise woman about it."

Curious, Simple asked, "And what did she say, sir?"

"She told me that the same man who tricked Master Slender out of his chain was the one who took it," Falstaff revealed.

Simple sighed, "I wish I could've spoken to her myself. Master Slender wanted me to ask her some other things too."

Falstaff was intrigued, "What things? Tell us."

The Innkeeper urged, "Yes, tell us quickly."

Simple hesitated, "I can't keep them secret, sir."

The Innkeeper, half-joking, threatened, "Tell us, or it'll be the worse for you."

. . .

Simple finally admitted, "Well, it was about Mistress Anne Page. Master wanted to know if he has a chance with her."

Falstaff confidently answered, "It is his fortune to have her."

Surprised, Simple asked, "Really, sir?"

"Yes," Falstaff nodded. "Go and tell your master that the woman said so."

Simple was grateful, "Thank you, sir. This will make my master very happy."

After Simple left, the Innkeeper turned to Falstaff, "You're quite the scholar, Sir John. Did you really have a wise woman with you?"

Falstaff laughed, "Oh yes, I did. She taught me more than I've ever learned before, and it didn't cost me a penny!"

Just then, Bardolph burst in, distressed, "Oh sir, it's been a disaster! The horses have been stolen by the tricksters. As soon as we got out of town, they threw me into the mud and rode off!"

. . .

The Innkeeper tried to stay calm, "They're just meeting the duke, don't worry. Germans are trustworthy."

Suddenly, Sir Hugh Evans appeared, warning the Innkeeper, "Be careful with your guests. There are three tricksters who have been cheating all the innkeepers around. I'm just telling you so you're aware."

Soon after, Doctor Caius came looking for the Innkeeper, "Where's the host? I heard there's a big welcome for a German duke. But there's no duke coming. Just letting you know."

The Innkeeper was in a panic, "Help, help! I've been tricked. Everybody, we need to find those thieves!"

Falstaff, left alone, mused, "I've been tricked and beaten. If the court hears of my misadventures, they'd laugh me out of town. I haven't had any luck since I gave up cheating at cards. I should probably repent."

Then, Mistress Quickly arrived, and Falstaff, frustrated with his recent troubles, lamented the hardship he's endured because of others' deceit and his own misfortune.

Falstaff had just finished sharing his woes when Mistress Quickly approached with news of her own. "Those poor ladies," she exclaimed. "Especially Mistress Ford! She's been treated so harshly she's covered in bruises."

Falstaff, feeling a bit self-pitying, responded, "Bruises? You're talking to someone who's been turned into a human rainbow of pain. I nearly ended up in jail, accused of being a witch, if not for my quick thinking and acting skills."

Mistress Quickly, eager to share more, suggested, "Let's talk more privately in your room. I've got a letter for you, and I think you'll be pleased with the news. It's been quite the task to get you two to meet. It seems like someone up there doesn't want you two getting along."

Intrigued and hoping for some good news at last, Falstaff agreed, "Let's go upstairs then." And with that, they both exited to continue their conversation in private.

SCENE 6

I n the Garter Inn, Fenton and the Host were deep in conversation. The Host, looking troubled, sighed heavily. "Master Fenton, I'm really worried today. I think I'm done helping out with things."

But Fenton, determined and hopeful, quickly said, "Please, just listen to what I have to say. I need your help with something very important. And I promise, I'll give you a nice reward for it."

The Host's interest was piqued, and he agreed to listen. "Alright, Master Fenton. I'll hear you out. And I'll keep your secret."

Fenton then shared his heart. "I've told you before how much I love Anne Page. She likes me back, just as much. I've got a letter from her that would amaze you. There's a funny plan involving Sir John Falstaff, but that's for later. Tonight, at Herne's oak, Anne is supposed to dress up as the Fairy Queen."

The Host leaned in, curious about the plan.

Fenton continued, "Her dad wants her to run away with Slender and marry him at once. But her mom wants her to marry Doctor Caius and has her own plan to sneak Anne away to marry him instead."

"And what does Anne want?" the Host asked, trying to keep up.

Fenton smiled. "She plans to fool them both and come away with me. But I need your help. Could you make sure the vicar is ready to marry us at the church, between twelve and one?"

The Host, now fully on board, nodded. "I'll talk to the vicar. Just make sure you bring Anne, and you won't miss having a priest."

Fenton's face lit up with gratitude. "Thank you! This means everything to me. I'll never forget your help, and I'll make sure to repay you."

. . .

With their plan in place and their spirits high, Fenton and the Host went their separate ways to prepare for the big event.

ACT V

SCENE I

In the cozy room of the Garter Inn, Falstaff waved his hand dismissively at Mistress Quickly. "Enough chit-chat, off you go. They say good fortune comes in threes, and this is our third try. Off I go!"

Mistress Quickly nodded, "I'll get you a chain, and try for those horns too."

Falstaff, growing impatient, urged, "Hurry, we're running out of time. Keep your chin up and let's move quickly." With that, Mistress Quickly left.

As she exited, Ford entered the scene, curious and anxious. "Falstaff, what's the news? Will we discover the truth tonight?"

. . .

"Yes, Master Brook," Falstaff responded with a twinkle in his eye. "Be in the park by midnight at Herne's oak. You're in for a show."

Ford, seeking confirmation, asked, "Did you visit her as you said you would?"

Falstaff chuckled, "Oh, I did. But I left feeling more like a doddering old woman than a man. That husband of hers, Ford, he's a wildly jealous one, let me tell you. He disguised himself and beat me, thinking I was someone else! But tonight, I plan my revenge. Come with me, and I'll fill you in on the way. We have much to prepare, and by the end, Mrs. Ford will be in your grasp."

Intrigued and eager, Ford agreed, and together they left the inn, plotting their next move under the cover of night.

SCENE 2

In the cool evening of Windsor Park, Page, along with his friends Shallow and Slender, prepared for an exciting adventure.

Page encouraged them with a twinkle in his eye, "Let's hide by the castle's ditch until the fairies appear. And remember, Slender, my daughter is part of our plan."

Slender nodded, eager to impress, "Yes, I've talked to her. We have a secret code. I'll wear white and say 'mum;' she'll reply 'budget.' That's how we'll recognize each other."

Shallow chuckled, finding the plan amusing yet simple, "That's clever. But honestly, wearing white is enough to find her. Look, it's already ten o'clock."

. . .

Page looked around at the darkening sky and felt the thrill of the night. "It's the perfect time for our fairy sport. As long as we're here for fun, nothing bad will happen. The only trouble-maker is the devil, and we'll spot him by his horns. Let's go, follow me."

And with that, the group vanished into the night, their hearts light with anticipation for the magical evening that lay ahead.

SCENE 3

Mistress Page and Mistress Ford were having a chat with Doctor Caius in the street leading to the park.

Mistress Page said, "Doctor, my daughter will be dressed in green. When it's the right time, take her hand, and quickly go with her to get married. You go ahead to the park; we will follow shortly."

Doctor Caius replied confidently, "I know what I must do. Goodbye."

"Goodbye, sir," Mistress Page wished him well as he left.

. . .

Once Doctor Caius was gone, Mistress Page shared a thought with Mistress Ford, "My husband won't be too happy about Doctor Caius marrying my daughter, but it's better than a lot of sadness."

Mistress Ford then wondered, "Where are Nan and her group of fairies, and Hugh, the Welsh mischief-maker?"

Mistress Page explained, "They're hiding near Herne's oak, with their lights off. As soon as Falstaff meets us, they'll light up the night."

"That will surely surprise him," Mistress Ford imagined.

Mistress Page nodded, "If he's not surprised, he'll be the joke of the night. And if he is surprised, he'll still end up being laughed at."

"We'll trick him so well," Mistress Ford chuckled.

Mistress Page agreed, "Tricking such naughty people is not wrong."

Mistress Ford excitedly suggested, "It's almost time. Let's head to the oak tree!"

. . .

And off they went to carry out their plan.

SCENE 4

In Windsor Park, Sir Hugh Evans dressed up like a fairy, along with his friends who were also dressed as fairies.

He whispered to them, excited, "Hurry, hurry, fairies; come along; and don't forget what you're supposed to do: be brave, please; follow me closely; and when I say the special words, do just as I've told you: come on, let's go, hurry, hurry."

And just like that, they all scampered off into the night, ready for their adventure.

SCENE 5

In a different part of the park, Falstaff had dressed up as Herne the Hunter and was waiting under the moonlight. The clock had just struck midnight, and he was feeling a mix of excitement and nerves.

"Oh, I hope the magical spirits help me now," Falstaff whispered to himself. "Remember how you, Jupiter, turned into a bull because you were in love? Love can do some strange things, turning us inside out and upside down. And then there was the time you became a swan. Love is truly a powerful force!"

He chuckled, thinking about the mischiefs of gods and their adventures in love. "Here I am, pretending to be a majestic stag in Windsor, hoping for a bit of that magical love luck. But, oh, what's a man to do when the gods themselves get into such mischief?"

Just then, Mistress Ford and Mistress Page arrived. Mistress Ford called out, "Sir John! Are you there, my dear, my brave deer?"

Falstaff replied with a smile, "Ah, my doe, welcome! I wish for a shower of potatoes, let thunder play our favorite tunes, and let it snow treats. If a storm of temptation arises, I'll stay right here for shelter."

"Mistress Page is here with me, dear," said Mistress Ford.

Falstaff, still in a playful mood, responded, "Then let's share this moment, like dividing a prize deer. I'll keep to myself, but offer my support to you both. Am I not the best at playing Herne the Hunter? Now, let's enjoy this magical night."

Suddenly, they heard some noises. Mistress Page whispered, "What's that sound?"

Mistress Ford, a bit anxious, said, "Let's hope it's nothing bad."

. . .

Falstaff, feeling a bit puzzled and scared, whispered, "What's happening now?"

Mistress Ford and Mistress Page, sensing trouble, quickly said, "We need to get out of here!" And with that, they hurried away.

Falstaff, half-joking, mumbled to himself, "I guess even the devil doesn't want me; I'd probably set fire to the place with all the mischief in me."

Suddenly, the night became even more magical and mysterious. Sir Hugh Evans, dressed as a fairy, along with Pistol as a Hobgoblin, Mistress Quickly, Anne Page, and others dressed as fairies, holding little lights, appeared.

Mistress Quickly started to call upon the fairies, "Fairies of all colors, creatures of the night and moonlight dancers, listen and do your duties."

Pistol, taking on his role, called out, "Fairies, gather and be quiet. Cricket, jump into Windsor's chimneys where you'll find unclean places, and pinch those who don't keep their homes clean, as our queen despises laziness and dirt."

. . .

Falstaff, realizing they were playing the roles of fairies, decided to lay low. "If I pretend to sleep, they won't bother me," he thought, so he laid down and closed his eyes.

Sir Hugh Evans gave further instructions, "Let's find those who are good and pray before they sleep, and let their dreams be sweet. But for those who forget their sins, let's pinch them as a reminder."

Mistress Quickly encouraged the fairies, "Let's spread good fortune throughout Windsor Castle, cleaning and blessing every corner, making everything pure and worthy of its owner. And let's not forget to sing and dance around Herne's oak at midnight, keeping our traditions alive."

Sir Hugh Evans, leading the playful troupe, said, "Let's join hands and form a line. We'll use glow-worms to light our way as we dance around the tree. But wait, I sense a human among us."

Falstaff, lying on the ground, thought to himself, "Oh, I hope that fairy doesn't turn me into cheese!"

Pistol, looking at Falstaff, said scornfully, "You were doomed from the start."

· · ·

Mistress Quickly had an idea, "Let's test him. If he's good, he won't feel the burn; but if he flinches, it means his heart isn't pure."

They all agreed to the test and touched Falstaff with their lights. Falstaff couldn't help but yell out in discomfort.

Mistress Quickly declared, "He's not pure at heart! Let's circle around him, singing and pinching him to teach him a lesson."

As they sang a song about the dangers of selfish desires and pinched Falstaff, chaos ensued. Doctor Caius, Slender, and Fenton took advantage of the distraction to carry out their own plans, each stealing away with someone dressed as a fairy. The sounds of a hunt startled everyone, and the fairies scattered.

Falstaff, finally removing his disguise and standing up, was then faced by Page, Ford, Mistress Page, and Mistress Ford, who had been watching the spectacle.

Page, with a hint of amusement, said, "There's no need to run. We've seen everything. Did you really think you could fool us with your act?"

. . .

Mistress Page asked, "What do you think of our little performance, Sir John? Do you see how well we played our parts?"

Ford, teasing Falstaff, said, "So, who's the fool now? You thought you were clever, but you ended up with nothing but trouble. And remember, you still owe Master Brook money for all the trouble you've caused."

As the moonlight danced through the trees, Sir John Falstaff found himself surrounded by what he believed were fairies. Mistress Ford spoke up, breaking the enchanting silence. "Sir John, it seems we've been quite unlucky. Despite our efforts, we never truly connected. Though I'll no longer consider you as my partner in love, you'll always be my dear 'deer' to me."

Feeling the weight of his foolishness, Falstaff sighed deeply. "It seems I've finally realized the joke's on me. I've been turned into a complete fool."

Ford couldn't help but add, "Indeed, you've been made both a fool and a laughingstock, all at once."

Falstaff, reflecting on the night's odd turn of events, shared his thoughts. "I was so convinced at times that these were not real fairies. Yet, somehow, the tricks played on my mind made me believe, against all sense and reason, that they were. It's astonishing how one's wit can be so easily duped when caught in mischief."

Sir Hugh Evans, seizing the moment to impart some wisdom, advised, "Sir John Falstaff, it would serve you well to devote yourself to God and abandon your wayward desires. Then, perhaps, the fairies will leave you be."

Ford praised Evans's wise counsel with a smile, "Well said, fairy Hugh."

"And let go of your jealousy while you're at it," Evans continued, hoping to guide Falstaff toward a better path.

Ford quipped with a chuckle, "I shall never doubt my wife again until you, Sir John, can woo her in perfect English."

Falstaff lamented over his gullibility. "Have I so lost my senses that I allowed myself to be so thoroughly tricked? Is my mind so parched for wisdom that I fell for such a blatant folly?"

Evans couldn't resist a playful jab, "Cheese and butter, Falstaff! Your thoughts are all mixed up."

. . .

Falstaff, bewildered by the evening's events and the jests at his expense, exclaimed, "To be mocked for my English by Evans! Has it come to this? Am I now a joke to be laughed at by all?"

Mistress Page, joining in the gentle rebuke, questioned Falstaff's earlier assumptions about their intentions. "Did you really think, Sir John, that with all the mischief and deception, you could ever be a source of delight for us?"

The group continued to tease Falstaff, comparing him to various unflattering things, emphasizing his many failings in a playful manner.

Falstaff, finally accepting his defeat, conceded to the group's amusement at his expense. "I see now that I am but the subject of your entertainment. Overwhelmed and outwitted, I have no response. You've seen through me, so do as you wish."

Ford, looking sternly at Falstaff, said, "Well, Sir, we'll be taking you to Windsor to meet Master Brook. You tricked him out of money, pretending to help him in ways you shouldn't have. And on top of everything you've been through, paying him back will be another tough lesson for you."

Page, trying to lighten the mood, chimed in with a chuckle, "Cheer up, Sir Knight. Tonight, you're invited to my house for a posset. It'll be a good time to share a laugh with my wife, who's having a good laugh at you right now. Tell her that Master Slender has married her daughter."

Mistress Page, puzzled and a bit worried, thought to herself, "That's doubtful. If Anne is indeed my daughter, she must be Doctor Caius' wife by now."

Suddenly, Slender rushed in, calling out excitedly, "Whoa ho! Father Page!"

Page, surprised, greeted him, "Son! What news? Have you done what you intended?"

Slender, almost out of breath, exclaimed, "Done? I'll have everyone in Gloucestershire talking about it! I went to Eton to marry Anne Page, and ended up with a big, clumsy boy! I was so confused; if it wasn't for the church setting, I might have ended up in a tussle with him."

Page shook his head, "Then you must have made a mistake."

Slender, frustrated, replied, "Of course, I made a mistake! I was expecting a girl, not a boy dressed in her clothes. Had I married him, it would have been a disaster, despite his disguise."

. . .

Page, trying to understand, asked, "Didn't I explain how to recognize my daughter by what she'd be wearing?"

Slender, still agitated, explained, "I looked for her in white, just as we planned. But it turned out to be a postmaster's boy, not Anne."

Mistress Page couldn't help but intervene, "George, please don't be upset. I knew about your plan and had Anne wear green instead. She's actually with Doctor Caius right now, and they are married."

Just then, Doctor Caius burst in, visibly upset, "Where is Mistress Page? By gar, I have been tricked: I married a boy, not Anne Page. I am utterly duped."

Mistress Page, puzzled, asked Doctor Caius, "Why did you pick the one in green?"

Doctor Caius, flustered and frustrated, replied, "Yes, and I ended up with a boy! I can't believe this happened. I'll have everyone in Windsor hear about this!" And with that, he stormed off.

Ford, scratching his head, said, "This is quite a mix-up. Who actually ended up marrying the real Anne Page?"

. . .

Just then, Fenton walked in with Anne Page, causing Page to ask eagerly, "What's going on, Master Fenton?"

Anne Page, looking a bit guilty but happy, pleaded, "Please forgive me, father, and you too, mother!"

Page, still confused, asked his daughter, "Why didn't you go with Master Slender?"

And Mistress Page, equally bewildered, asked, "And why not with Doctor Caius?"

Fenton, stepping forward to explain, said, "Let me clear things up. You all had plans that didn't include what Anne or I wanted. We've been in love and promised to each other for a long time. What happened today wasn't trickery, but us choosing our own path away from forced marriages."

Ford, realizing the situation, advised, "There's nothing we can do about it now. In matters of love, sometimes the stars decide for us. Money might buy land, but fate decides on love."

. . .

Falstaff, finding a silver lining in the chaos, commented, "I'm just relieved that even though everyone was aiming at me, I've managed to dodge the worst of it."

Page, finally accepting the situation, wished Fenton joy, "What can't be avoided must be accepted."

Falstaff added philosophically, "At the end of the day, all sorts of unexpected things can happen."

Mistress Page decided it was time to move on, "No more dwelling on this. Congratulations, Master Fenton. Let's all head home and share a laugh over this by the fire."

Ford agreed, "Yes, let's do that. And Sir John, you're not off the hook yet. You've still got a promise to keep to Master Brook."

And with that, they all decided to head home, leaving the night's confusions and mix-ups behind them, ready to enjoy a good laugh and the warmth of a country fire.

THE END

THE MERRY WIVES OF WINDSOR: A TALE OF MIRTH AND MISCHIEF

Reflecting on "The Merry Wives of Windsor," this play offers a tapestry of humor, wit, and Elizabethan social commentary, woven with characters and situations that sparkle with life and laughter. As we reach the end of this delightful journey, let's uncover some intriguing facts and subtle nuances that enrich our understanding of this Shakespearean comedy.

Falstaff's Return: Sir John Falstaff, the boisterous and lovable rogue, is one of the few characters in Shakespeare's works who appears in multiple plays. Originally featured in the Henry IV plays, his popularity likely inspired Shakespeare to bring him back for "The Merry Wives of Windsor." This time, Falstaff's adventures are centered not on political machinations but on domestic and romantic entanglements, showcasing a different facet of his character.

. . .

A Play on Demand: Legend has it that Queen Elizabeth I was so amused by Falstaff that she requested Shakespeare to write another play featuring him, specifically wanting to see Falstaff in love. Whether this tale is apocryphal or not, "The Merry Wives of Windsor" indeed presents a unique exploration of Falstaff's character in a more personal and less heroic context.

A Glimpse into Elizabethan Life: Unlike many of Shakespeare's plays that are set in distant lands and royal courts, "The Merry Wives of Windsor" offers a rare look into the middle-class life of Elizabethan England. The setting and social dynamics provide insights into the customs, humor, and daily concerns of the time, making the play a valuable snapshot of contemporary life.

Language and Localization: This play stands out for its use of contemporary English, rather than the more formal verse found in Shakespeare's other works. The dialogue includes a mix of prose and vernacular speech, making it more accessible to audiences of Shakespeare's time and adding to its comedic effect. The inclusion of characters like Dr. Caius and Sir Hugh Evans adds a touch of linguistic diversity, reflecting the multicultural makeup of Elizabethan society.

Themes of Honor and Wit: At its heart, "The Merry Wives of Windsor" is a celebration of cleverness and virtue over deceit and pomposity. The play champions the intelligence and resourcefulness of women, a progressive theme for its time. The triumph of Mistress Page and Mistress Ford over Falstaff's schemes reinforces the idea that honor and wit can prevail over folly and vice.

The Fairy Finale: The play concludes with a fantastical fairy scene, a departure from the realism that characterizes much of the narrative. This whimsical ending not only serves as poetic justice for Falstaff but also allows for a communal celebration that unites the characters. It's a reminder of the power of imagination and the importance of community and forgiveness.

A Mirror to Society: Through its characters and plot, "The Merry Wives of Windsor" reflects the complexities of social status, marriage, and gender dynamics. The play subtly critiques societal norms while also affirming the values of loyalty, friendship, and social harmony. It encourages the audience to laugh not only at the characters' foibles but also at the universal human condition.

As we close the curtain on "The Merry Wives of Windsor," we're left with a richly layered comedy that entertains while offering insights into human nature and Elizabethan society. Shakespeare's ability to blend humor with social commentary ensures that the play remains relevant and engaging, inviting audiences to discover new layers and lessons with each viewing.

THE LIFE OF WILLIAM SHAKESPEARE

S tep back in time with us as we discover the exciting life of **William Shakespeare**—a storyteller whose magnificent tales have been told and retold for hundreds of years. Fasten your seatbelts for some amazing facts about the Bard of Avon!

Birthday Mystery: Believe it or not, we don't know exactly when Shakespeare was born. Historians guess it was around April 23, 1564, but that's all because of the date of his baptism. How curious that such a famous person has a birthday shrouded in mystery!

School Days: Young Shakespeare attended the King's New School in his hometown, where he learned important subjects like Latin, Greek, history, and poetry—all without the gadgets and technology students have today.

. . .

Word Wizard: Shakespeare had a way with words, inventing over 1,700 of them! Imagine, every time you say "bedroom" or "excitement," you're using words that Shakespeare introduced to the English language.

Globe Trotter - But Not Really: The Globe Theatre is where Shakespeare's masterpieces were first performed—not a globe you can spin, but a large, round, open-air theater where audiences marveled under the sky.

Super-sized Works: Our dear Bard wrote 37 plays and 154 sonnets. That's a lot of storytelling! If you wrote a poem every week of the year, you'd still be short of Shakespeare's sonnet count.

Nicknamed "The Bard": Shakespeare is often referred to as "The Bard of Avon." 'Bard' means poet, and indeed, Shakespeare was a master poet from the town of Stratford-upon-Avon.

Lovey-Dovey Lines: Shakespeare's words about love are so beautiful that they are still read at weddings and shared between sweethearts today. And if you've heard the phrase "to be or not to be," you're quoting one of his most famous lines!

. . .

Queen for a Fan: Queen Elizabeth I loved the theater, and Shakespeare's plays were some of her most enjoyed performances. It was quite the honor for Shakespeare to entertain her majesty with his work.

Shakespeare's Secret Code: Some folks believe that Shakespeare tucked away secret codes within his plays—making each performance not just a show, but also a puzzle full of hidden meanings.

Goodnight, Sweet Prince: At age 52, in the year 1616, Shakespeare took his final bow. His presence may be missed, but his stories live on, continuing to inspire, entertain, and provoke thought across the globe.

So there you have it—a little peek into the life of the man who has kept us company through his words for over four centuries. Open the pages of his stories, and let William Shakespeare's plays transport you to a world where imagination knows no bounds. Happy reading!

ABOUT THE AUTHOR

Jeanette Vigon is a vibrant storyteller hailing from the sun-kissed beaches of California, where her Spanish heritage infuses her writing with a colorful zest for life. Born to Spanish immigrants who carried stories of their homeland across the ocean, Jeanette's childhood was rich with tales that sparked her imagination and sowed the seeds for her future in storytelling.

After completing her education with a focus on early childhood development, Jeanette dedicated herself to the noble profession of teaching. As a beloved primary school teacher, she spent years enlightening young minds in the classroom. Her magical ability to turn even the most mundane lesson into a memorable adventure earned her admiration from both her pupils and peers.

However, the call of the pen proved too strong for Jeanette to ignore. Diving headfirst into the world of literature, she transitioned from shaping minds with chalk to enchanting them with words as a full-time writer. Her intimate knowledge of children's learning styles, combined with her rich cultural roots, enables her to craft stories that are not only engaging but also educational.

Jeanette's writing is characterized by its empathy, humor,

and a deep understanding of what captivates children's hearts and minds. Whether retelling a classic Shakespearean tale or penning an original story, her books are beloved for their ability to bridge cultural gaps and bring diverse experiences to the forefront of children's literature.

Now, with several acclaimed titles to her name, Jeanette continues to share her passion for enriching young lives through reading. When she's not lost in her latest manuscript, you can find her indulging in her love for travel, exploring new destinations, and collecting fresh inspirations for her next enchanting narrative.

It's hard for books to get noticed these days.
Whether you liked this one or not, please consider
writing a review, thanks!

Jeanette Vigon

SHAKESPEARE FOR KIDS
- OTHER BOOKS IN THE
SERIES

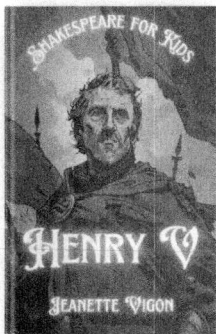

You can find the rest of the books in the series here:

https://amzn.to/3wLXpTC

Printed in Great Britain
by Amazon

42949518R00116